BROKEN HOMES

BRITAIN'S HOUSING CRISIS

Faults, Factoids and Fixes

Peter Bill and Jackie Sadek

Matador
9 Priory Business Park,
Wistow Road, Kibworth Beauchamp,
Leicestershire. LE8 0RX
Tel: 0116 279 2299
Email: books@troubador.co.uk
Web: www.troubador.co.uk/matador
Twitter: @matadorbooks

ISBN 978 1800460 379

British Library Cataloguing in Publication Data.
A catalogue record for this book is available from the British Library.

Printed and bound by CPI Group (UK) Ltd, Croydon, CR0 4YY
Typeset in 12pt Adobe Jenson Pro by Troubador Publishing Ltd, Leicester, UK

Matador is an imprint of Troubador Publishing Ltd

For
Anna, Emilia and Elsa
&
Alfred and Theodore

'Our broken housing market is one of the greatest barriers to progress in Britain today. Whether buying or renting, the fact is that housing is increasingly unaffordable – particularly for ordinary working-class people who are struggling to get by.' **Theresa May, Prime Minister**
Fixing our broken housing market, February '17

'Over the years, the response from politicians has been piecemeal. Well-intentioned initiatives have built more homes here and there but have skirted around the edges of a growing problem. That has to change. We need radical, lasting reform.' **Sajid Javid, Housing Secretary**
Fixing our broken housing market, February '17

'Not more fiddling around the edges, not simply painting over the damp patches, but levelling the foundations and building, from the ground up, a whole new planning system for England.'

Boris Johnson, Prime Minister
Planning for the Future, August 2020

'These proposals will help build the homes our country needs, bridge the generational divide and recreate an ownership society in which more people have the dignity and security of a home of their own.'

Robert Jenrick, Secretary of State for Housing
Planning for the Future, August 2020

'How the government seeks to reach collective agreement on these things can be completely dysfunctional.'

Gavin Barwell, Housing Minister 2016/17
Chapter Three, Faults and Factoids

'I fundamentally believe we have answers to the country's housing crisis and the government does not.'

John Healey, former Shadow Housing Secretary
Chapter Three, Faults and Factoids

INTRODUCTION

Peter Bill

When Jackie remarked that she wanted to write a book on the broken housing market, and I agreed to help, the first thing she said was 'we mustn't fall out'. It is not possible to fall out with a woman of such warmth, energy and fun. I had thought that my 2014 book *Planet Property*, about the commercial real estate sector, would be my last. But the chance to examine the malfunctioning machine that supplies new homes, both private and public, in such spirited company was irresistible. Having spent a decade at what was plain George Wimpey, followed by a decade at *Building* magazine, then another at *Estates Gazette*, I felt I had an ancient but working knowledge of the sector, and had learned the trick of finding things out and writing them down.

Fixes for the planning system have been largely avoided in *Broken Homes*. The idea that repairing the pipework will produce more water is a conceit best left to those mistaken enough to think it will alter the laws of supply and demand. But the attempt by the government in August 2020 to at least try and increase the supply of land via proposals in the 'Planning for the Future' white paper deserves inclusion.

What has not had attention before is the disregard of planners, designers and builders for those who buy or rent new homes. A world where homes are crammed to meet targets, where occupants are forced to fit, rather than form, the mould. Where the desire for decent-sized homes is being thwarted by rules that encourage matchbox estates. A world in which the role of a home changed forever in the 2020 pandemic, but where space standards are no higher than 100 years ago.

Nor has the short-term, haphazard and partisan development of housing policy by government been exposed before. How political misadventures have led to the housing crisis Britain faces today. Former Conservative and Labour housing ministers interviewed for *Broken Homes* freely admit to a dysfunctional system presiding over ill-formed plans mainly pushed by partisan lobby groups.

The fallacy that building more homes will bring down prices has remained unchallenged until now. As has the 'factoid' that the crisis is the fault of planners or housebuilders. Or that improving the planning system will make any difference. Instead, decent-sized decently spaced homes can be demanded by government, which must also face the fact that they need to subsidise a major programme to build homes for those who will never be able to pay more than half the market rent.

There is, of course, no one 'silver bullet' to solve the housing crisis. Jackie Sadek fires her shots at the end of Chapter Ten. Raise minimum space standards. Lower maximum density levels. Make both mandatory. Put people first not land values, even if it is just in a new generation of new towns. Accept Oliver Letwin's proposal to change the 1961 Land Compensation Act to put a ceiling of ten times existing use value on brownfield and farmland granted permission for homes. Finally, accept the idea that only a mass building programme which delivers homes rented in perpetuity at half market rents is the only way to alleviate the plight of those that will never get to step on the housing ladder and buy.

Broken Homes was completed in August 2020, as the coronavirus pandemic continued. The prime minister, Boris Johnson, was urging the country to 'build, build, build' ahead of introducing 'Planning for the Future' a plan based on the mistaken assumption that changing the planning system would bring 300,000 new homes a year. 'Not more fiddling around the edges, not simply painting over the damp patches, but levelling the foundations and building, from the ground up, a whole new planning system for England.' The execution of these ideas will play out over the next five to ten years.

PB

Jackie Sadek

In February 2016, I took a super difficult decision. As a result, I handed in my notice to Greg Clark, then Secretary of State for Communities and Local Government, to return to run the company I had helped found in 2010 – UKR Regeneration. It was difficult because working in Greg's private office, on his brilliant devolution and local growth agenda, was the best job I had ever had. But I was becoming increasingly drawn towards the housing crisis.

I was beginning to feel that it was wholly untenable to continue to expend my (increasingly in shorter supply) energies on running around the country, telling people what to do from Whitehall. I felt that the only way I could *genuinely* help sort the housing crisis – and, for good measure, whilst we were there, all the other ills of the mainly dismal modern built environment scene – was to get back out there and demonstrate exactly *how* to do it. Show them what good looks like. I wanted to stop talking about it and start doing it. I do apologise for the hubris.

So, I left the civil service after three very rewarding years and I returned to my company, UKR. To bastardise the famous quote from Mrs Patrick Campbell, it was like leaving the deep peace of the marriage bed to return to the hurly-burly of the chaise longue. The story of UKR (roughly a game of two halves) is captured in Chapter Eight. As we relate, breaking into property development is seriously hard. It's been a long old haul to get to here and, at the time of writing, whilst we may have reached the tipping point, we still haven't put a spade in the ground on our Biggleswade site.

In July 2019, my old friend, venerable journalist Peter Bill (who has held my hand throughout this ten-year journey), took me for lunch at the Reform Club – as one does! We reprised our regular hand-wringing conversation about the housing crisis. And I told him that I wanted to capture the UKR story, as a worked example of how it has come about. By that stage, I had succeeded in getting an outline planning permission for 1,500 homes, but it had been a very painful trajectory. There and then we hatched the idea for *Broken Homes*. The result is this book, full of clever analysis about the housing crisis – for which I can take not a lot of credit; it is mostly the work of my learned co-author. We were fortunate to be able to mine Peter's invaluable archive of his columns in the *Evening Standard* and *Estates Gazette*, as well as in *Planning* and *Property Week*, together with his work for the Smith Institute think tank – not to mention his formidable memory. We were fortunate in being able to interview a lot of leading thinkers in the housing industry. But underpinning all of this work, *Broken Homes* is informed throughout – factually and emotionally – by the UKR story and the sheer reality of how bloody hard it is to do anything out there. Bailey Park is, but of course, a thinly disguised proxy for the leafy villages that UKR proposes for the east of Biggleswade. The greatest (and most under-sung) hero of this tale is the magical and mystical Jason Blain, the visionary co-founder of UKR; if UKR succeeds in our mission it will be entirely down to his unswerving belief and stamina.

A mutual friend once described Peter and me as 'the Odd Couple'. Guilty as charged. But I take the view (again, perhaps a tad hubristically) that we are a unique pairing of folk to try to tackle this subject. Peter worked for a housebuilder for a decade and has been commenting on the market for further decades. And I am out there trying to change things – living out my life's dream – desperately trying to disrupt the development industry and build something very much better for ordinary people. Needless to say, *Broken Homes* became something of a polemic! For that, I will not apologise.

JS

ACKNOWLEDGEMENTS

We would like to recognise all who contributed their time, wisdom, comments and perspectives. Without their aid, *Broken Homes* would be filled with many more bloopers than it still contains. Mentions in dispatches? First, four former housing ministers, Gavin Barwell, Mark Prisk, Nick Raynsford and John Healey for their interviews; also to Barratt Developments director of Land and Planning, Philip Barnes, who corrected many misconceptions in drafts of the first two chapters, and provided valuable insight in Chapter Seven on how housebuilders operate; also to space standards expert, Julia Park, for reading drafts of Chapter Four – 'Ghosts in the Machine', and for permission to reprint her reports uncovering the shocking conditions endured by families living in 'homes' built under Permitted Development Rights; also to Toby Lloyd, former head of policy at Shelter and housing advisor at 10 Downing Street, whose insight into the development of housing policy, the skirmishes over land value tax – and a deep understanding of the social housing sector – was invaluable.

Broken Homes would be an empty house without the help and support offered to Jackie Sadek on the journey UK Regeneration has been on for a decade. For that reason, the list of acknowledgements includes both those who have contributed to *Broken Homes* and to aiding UKR's journey. This alphabetic list is necessarily long.

Thank you all:

John Assael, John Badman, Liam Bailey, Philip Barnes, Gavin Barwell, Isobel Battock, Simon Bayliss, Lizzie Bill, Tom Bill, David

Birkbeck, Jason Blain, Tim Bottrill, Rob Bower, Nicholas Boys Smith, Sue Brown, Adrian Bunnis, Mike Burton, Robin Butler, Cormac Byrne, Deborah Cadman, Greg Callaghan, Jude Carter, Adam Challis, Greg Clark, Amy Coleman, Kevin Collins, Lucian Cook, James Corcoran, Martin Crookston, Tony Danaher, Colin Danks, Jimmy Denholm, Ben Derbyshire, Tom Dobson, Charles Dugdale, Manu Dwivedi, Andy Evans, Judith Evans, Paul Evans, Mark Farmer, Paul Finch, Digby Flower, Tim Garratt, Susan Geddes, Dominic Gibson, Simon Goldstein, Helen Gordon, Piers Gough, Bill Grimsey, Robert Grundy, Ben Gummer, John Gummer, Paul Hackett, Richard Hall, Liz Hamson, Michelle Hannah, Richard Hannay, Leona Hannify, Derek Harris, Tracey Hartley, John Healey, Giles Heather, Ian Henderson, Michael Heseltine, Ingrid Hooley, Martyn Horne, Nigel Hugill, Marc Humphrey, Andy Hunt, Sid Iyer, Heather Jameson, James Jamieson, Brendan Jarvis, Liz Jenkins, Marcus Jones, Andrew Kavanagh, Jonathan Kelly, Daniel Keys, Paul Kitson, Felicie Krikler, Tim Leathes, Brandon Lewis, Stuart Lipton, Ed Lister, Ben Lloyd, Toby Lloyd, Jason Longhurst, James Lord, Simon Lyons, Gill Marshall, Dominic Martin, Sam McClary, Chloe McCulloch, Adrian Montague, Trevor Moross, Steve Moseley, Stuart Nissen, Peter Padden, Julia Park, Kevin Parker, PK Patel, Eva Pascoe, Liz Peace, Robert Pilcher, Mark Prisk, Nick Raynsford, Jonathan Rosenberg, Archie Russell, Madeline Russell and all at Biggleswade Town Council, Elizabeth Sadek, Grant Shapps, Chris Shellard, Alan J. Smith, Eric Sorensen, Andrew Stanford, Wendy Stanton, Wilf Stevenson, Alastair Stewart, Deirdre Taylor, Steve Thomas, Simon Topliss, Tom Walker, Nick Walkley, Clare Waller, Ralph Ward, David Waterhouse, Stefan Webb, Damian Wild, Alex Williams, Bob Woollard, Nigel Young.

We also place on record our debt of gratitude to friends and mentors, sadly no longer with us: Alan Cherry, Geoff Marsh, Tony Pidgley and John Sienkiewicz.

Bibliography

We decided not to include a bibliography in this opus. This was mainly because you could suffocate under the drifts of literature there is on housing. But we would suggest six go-to sources if you are seeking further enlightenment. The first would be 'New Civic Housebuilding' produced by Shelter in 2017. The second would be 'Fixing Our Broken Housing Market', the 2017 Housing White Paper produced by the May administration. The third would be Sir Oliver Letwin's 'Independent review of build-out', from 2018, which includes fresh ideas for capturing land values. Fourth would be the 2020 'Living with Beauty' report from the Building Better, Building Beautiful Commission; particularly the Knight Frank addendum reports 'Building in Beauty' and 'Cost and Value' referred to at the end of Chapter Two. The fifth and sixth documents are those produced by right of the centre think tank, Policy Exchange. The first, 'Rethinking the Planning System for the 21st Century', published in January 2020. The second, 'Planning Anew', a collection of essays published in June 2020. This final pair of publications provided the intellectual underpinning for the August 2020 'Planning for the Future' White Paper.

CONTENTS

CHAPTERS ONE AND TWO

PREFACE

The following paired chapters take their titles and some inspiration from Frank Capra's 1946 film, *It's a Wonderful Life*. A tear-jerker starring James Stewart, as George Bailey, the idealistic developer of 'Bailey Park', a planned estate of decent homes for workers in Bedford Falls, archetypal small-town America. The Bad Guy, Henry F. Potter (Lionel Barrymore), is a slum landlord who rigs fraud charges against George. Our principled hero is driven to the edge of suicide, lamenting he wished he'd never been born.

As George is about to throw himself off a bridge, ageing apprentice angel Clarence appears. Clarence conjures up visions of Potter's Field: a dystopian settlement, populated by bitter, disappointed folk, gambling, drinking and fighting. 'This is what Bedford Falls would have looked like if you had not lived,' says Clarence. Chastened by this spectre, George rallies. He vanquishes Potter. All ends happily.

Bailey Park and Potter's Field

A mythical 100-hectare plot of land on the outskirts of (the real) Bedford is used to braid the political, planning and financial strands into a narrative that tries to explain the forces that can either mould development for the better or warp it for the worse. Bailey Park is moulded by the forces of good in the shape of an idealistic George Bailey. Potter's Field is warped, not by evil, rather by the very real pressures imposed on all housebuilders, good or bad. What is also faked are the lives of the Ghost family, Lulu and Ryan, placed in the narrative in an admittedly wooden and perhaps exaggerated fashion to try and give a little life to those generally disregarded by professionals.

Not faked

What is not faked in both chapters are the numbers. Development appraisal models were constructed for both the 1,500 homes George builds in Chapter One at 'Bailey Park' and the 2,000 units imagined by less altruistic Nook Homes at Potter's Field. The figures were run through a modelling programme by planners Montagu Evans. The appraisals have been kept simplistic but should give non-experts a view of how the moving parts relate, particularly on the impact on land values of taking a more idealistic approach. Real-world house prices and financing costs as of 2020 are used. The £233 million construction cost in the appraisal (page 9) at Bailey Park is made up from £168 million of build costs for the 1.4 million square feet of homes and flats, priced at £110 per square foot for the houses and £130 per square foot for the flats, plus a 5% contingency. The estimate for infrastructure and external works is £65 million. The 25% smaller units at Potter's Field mean the floor areas are similar. Here, the £248 million construction cost in the appraisal (page 31) is made up of £173 million of build costs and £75 million for infrastructure and external works.

Real world

By chance, Knight Frank was having similar thoughts. At the end of Chapter Two, there is a report on Fineborough: an imaginary development on the outskirts of an imaginary town. An account used to demonstrate the real-world trials of developing new homes on a large scale with the intent to build better. Knight Frank also provide real-world examples of how higher prices can offset the cost of building more beautifully.

ONE

BAILEY PARK

'Some see things the way they should be and ask why not?'
George Bernard Shaw

Part one: the Ghost family

The Ghost family moved to Bailey Park in 2030. Ryan and Lulu were newly married, both earning, so just able to afford a three-bed semi for £328,000 at the head of an unfinished cul-de-sac. Around 10% of the 1,500 homes planned on the eastern outskirts of Bedford had been built. Ten years on, in 2040, Bailey Park is pretty much complete, if still a little raw. Buyers like what they see. Demand for resales is steady; prices are 10–15% higher than on rival new estates.

Estate agents described Bailey Park as being 'popular and favoured'. A sense of community had developed, especially among those whose children attended the new school, which attained Ofsted-outstanding status in 2037. By 2040 the catchment area at Bailey Primary had shrunk to the boundaries of the development. Couples who moved in during the early thirties stayed to raise families, or 'traded up' on the estate for more bedrooms. Owners were building extensions and adding conservatories, rather than moving out. The avenue of trees on the 'boulevard' spine road were beginning to mature. Those who lived in Bailey Park said so with a touch of pride.

Spacious home

Ryan and Lulu's home was spacious. Two people could pass in the hall. There was room for a pushchair. Lulu's parents had been happy to stump up £30,000 towards the cost, after taking a look round at what else was on offer locally. They rather wanted grandchildren. Her father had a robust way with him. 'You have got a nice garden, front and back – and a drive to park two cars. Not like that poky little Nook box down the road. Our conservatory's bigger than the ruddy back garden. The front doors open straight on to the road! One designated parking spot! How long before you are fighting with the neighbours over where to park Lulu's car?'

The developers at Bailey Park had given each of the houses at least two parking spaces on their plot. The three- and four-bed private homes all had garages as well. These tended to be used as storage space for the *stuff* families accumulate: bikes, scooters, barbecue sets, that old table-tennis table. The garage was also a popular spot to hide the rubbish bins, which folk in the terraces had to stand in their front garden. The coming of electric cars meant buyers were prepared to pay a premium to recharge from their mains. Charging points in allotted or communal spaces used by those in the flats were more expensive and prone to being vandalised.

Ryan and Lulu were also sold by what they called 'the toot room' – what tweedy country-folk would call a boot room. In this case, a cupboard, just inside the front door. Big enough to take numerous pairs of shoes, coats, scarves, hats, the odd skateboard, plus the backpacks you need to find space for with three children. By 2040, Ryan and Lulu had three under the age of ten. Lulu worked part-time in the community centre, built by developers next to the parade of shops. Ryan had bagged one of their three bedrooms as a place to work. Few people commuted every day. They had to build an extension out into the back garden when their third child came along in 2038. Fortunately, there was room. Ryan now sat out there on Mondays and Fridays, the days he worked from home.

Not all wonderful

It was not all 'a wonderful life' at Bailey Park. Everyone agreed the housing association flats and terraces were a bit of an eyesore; all lumped together by the busy ring road. Ryan and Lulu had younger friends in one of the 'social' terraces. It seemed pinched. Still, their friends were glad to have a fresh new home at a rent they could afford. Those up by the ring road tended to keep to themselves, which disappointed Ryan and Lulu, who were sold on the idea of a 'mixed community', as the brochure had put it delicately. Would it not have been better to properly mix things up, they thought? Idealistic architects had called for 'pepper-potting', in the early days of mixed estates. But housing associations found it cheaper to keep their flocks in blocks, which could then be more easily managed.

Similar thoughts went through their heads when it came to the private flats clustered around and over the shopping parade. A flat rented by a couple Ryan and Lulu got to know was lovely. A bit small. Still, they commuted to London every day, so it didn't matter. These flats had quite posh communal areas. But Ryan's friends said those who used these spaces tended to be the short-term renters looking for company. Lulu felt these younger folks gave life to Bailey Park. She just wished they stayed a bit longer. Never mind, everyone loved having older folk in the retirement homes. Hard to get away from when you went to the shops. But, along with those with school-age children, they were the heart of the community.

Part two: George Bailey's journey

George Bailey's social conscience had been formed by his Quaker parents. Eleanor and Peter became fond of Frank Capra's 1946 film *It's a Wonderful Life* during its 1980s renaissance. The fight for the soul of home-town America is played out in 'Bedford Falls', a clash between principled developer George Bailey and wicked landlord Henry Potter. Bailey fought to build decent homes for the workers renting Potter's slums. A plan to build 'Bailey Park' on the outskirts of town was initially thwarted by Potter. When Eleanor and Peter's son was born in 1985 it seemed right to name him George, as their surname was Bailey.

2007–22

George got a job with Nook Homes in 2007, after leaving Reading University aged twenty-two, with an MSc in development. As a fast-track graduate trainee, he circulated through sales, marketing and buying, before being appointed as a land manager, based in Oxford. He soon moved up to become land director for the Beds, Bucks and Oxon region in Luton. By 2015, aged thirty, George was Nook's regional manager, in charge of building homes as well as buying land.

Feeding Nook's land bank took a lot of his time. The business, founded by Sir Ron Pinchup in 1985, was selling 10,000 units a year by 2007. A rolling three-year strategic plan guided every decision. 'You can't plan one year ahead when it might take three to get permission,' said Sir Ron, rather too often. 'Means we have 30,000 units in the pipeline.' Nook had its own land buyers, supplemented by a semi-official network of commission agents, whose main task was to identify sites no one else had yet spotted, not just using the information in the public domain. Everybody saw that: more, an informal chat with planning officers, or buying locals a few pints in the pub. The more sophisticated would drive around the district in a four-by-four with a savvy planning consultant, scanning fields that one day may be zoned for homes.

If Nook unearthed likely 'White Land', as Sir Ron still called it, the owner was approached with an 'option' offer, a smallish sum of money, plus, 'stick with us, we'll try and get planning and will share the gains in land value with you'. Nook was happy to take a ten- or even fifteen-year bet that planning might be granted. Plenty of these bets never paid off. But, if they did the deal went something like this: 'After we get planning, we both get the site valued. Once we agree on the value, we pay you X% of that value, minus the cost of us getting permission.'

George was often offered what in modern-day parlance is called 'strat-land' at Nook. What became Bailey Park was offered to George in 2020. The man offering the site was Neil Grabbier, a land surveyor that George knew well from his uni days. So, he pushed it on up the line.

Nook looked

The 100 hectares turned out to be too big a bite for Nook. The local planners hinted 2,000 units might be acceptable, which worked out at close to thirty to the hectare on the seventy hectares on which you could actually build houses. The rest was given over to the spine road, parks, a school and a 'village centre'. Nook's appraisal team ran the numbers. Out popped the estimate of what's called the residual land value. Arrived at by using a simple formula: income plus profit, minus expenditure, is what you can afford to pay for the land. Complex mathematics buzzes away in the background. Formulae used to calculate income and expenditure over time. In this case fifteen years. Nook found it could go to £43 million for the site, a figure depressed by £40 million – a guess at what the council would want for a school, community centre and any other pet project they had in mind.

Guessing the quantum of these 'Planning Obligations' was tricky. They have to be negotiated in parallel with trying to get permission, during which time both sides have to pretend there is no conflict. Nook's final offer for the land was never made until they were certain of these costs. Nook guessed it would take five years to have full permission and the planning obligations settled. Then another ten to build out the £500 million settlement. Too much time, too much risk of a recession, Nook said no. The land lay fallow for a few years. But George could not ignore his instinct and kept the appraisal on his personal laptop, just in case.

2023–25

In the late teens, the government's National Infrastructure Commission suggested one million new homes could be built along a new rail link between Oxford and Cambridge via Milton Keynes. The line transcribed a curve. The concept of an 'Arc' of opportunity was formed. In 2020, the government promised four new development corporations would be set up to build new towns along the Arc. Later, a station was promised close to the site Grabbier had spotted. George turned thirty-eight in 2023. An ambition to do things his way arose. He had become disillusioned at Nook. The focus on sales and driving down costs had got to George. He felt the customers came a poor third. Complainants were beginning to get on his nerves. Then a complaint came that was a little too close to home for comfort.

Past sins

One evening in April 2023, he visited a site of seventy-five homes Nook had built on a 2.5-hectare site near Marlow. George went at the behest of one of his site managers, Ken, whose daughter Kate and her partner Colin had bought a three-storey terrace in 2018. 'Take a look at what we are doing to people,' he said. On arrival, George's first thought was, *Where the hell am I going to park?* Cars and vans jammed the close. Many with wheels up on rutted verges. George remembered the layouts and the Computer Generated Images in the marketing brochure showing verges filled with flowers and bushes.

Two steps from the kerb was the front door. 'Come inside.' Kate smiled, stepping back into the living-room doorway to let George squeeze past into the narrow room. 'Colin and I loved this house when we bought it five years ago. We knew it was small, but new is so nice. The smell! No chain. Colin and I were working. Neither of us likes gardening. The back garden is the size of a table-tennis table. That didn't seem to matter. Nook put down the decking for free!'

Why am I here? thought George. Kate answered his unspoken question. 'You shouldn't build stuff this close. I've got a two-year-old and another on the way. Everyone has two cars. The carpenter next door has a van as well. We have one allocated space. But there is constant hassle over where people put their second vehicle. About eight vans and half a dozen motorbikes park up each night. We have three bins. All lined up by the front door. Didn't show that on the brochure, did you?' George began to see. 'I want to bring up my family in a place with unclogged roads, where it is safe to play, where we have a garden and a place to park our car on the drive,' said Kate. 'With space out back to build an extension if we feel like it. We can't stay here.'

Colin and Kate were moving to a nearby 1980s estate. 'We will have a garden. A drive. A garage, even. The kids can play in the cul-de-sac and walk to school or the park, or the local shops when they are older. We want to live somewhere we can put down roots, become part of the community, and yes, stay till we get older. Do you know what sticks in the craw? We've been here for five years. The price of older houses around here has gone up. We've been offered less than we paid you! Why don't you build houses that people can live in for more than a few years? Must be more money in it, surely?'

The germ of an idea

A few weeks earlier Neil Grabbier had called. He was still running a small land scouting business, using shell companies to put down options on behalf of housebuilders who did not want to show their hand. 'You know that land Nook looked at a few years ago?' he said. 'Well, it looks like the farmer is trying to sell again. It's on the books of a couple of agricultural agents. Does Nook want another go?

'No,' said George, then, after a long pause, 'but I might.' He knew the council was ashamed of a nearby 'matchbox' estate, where homes were being squeezed on at thirty-two to the hectare. Lowered the tone. He wondered if there might be a chance of persuading them to grant permission on the condition of building bigger, more widely spaced homes? He didn't want to go much above twenty to the hectare. George had studied the Essex Design Guide, a book of exemplar layouts originated by an enlightened county council.

He especially liked the 'Boulevard' layouts shown in the guide. These showed lots of room for trees, at twenty homes per hectare. He remembered homes could only be built on seventy of the 100 hectares. Fine: seventy hectares at twenty-one to the hectare would give him nearly 1,500 homes, a density that would allow 25% larger homes.

Laptop exercise

George wanted out from Nook, but not without a plan. He fired up the old Nook appraisal on his laptop and began to fiddle. Meanwhile, he set Neil Grabbier to work – undercover. He promised Neil a thin slice of the equity, in return. First, to search the Land Registry looking for hidden snags. Then to sew up the farmer with an option agreement. Then to trawl the publicly available planning information, to get a feel for the likelihood of getting permission. But, most importantly, to find if the council was amenable to bigger homes at lower densities. The more homes the better thought most councils. George was determined to put no more than 1,500 units on the land, allowing him to spread them far enough apart to give space for gardens and trees. He had his vision and was going to stick with it.

This undercover work took quite a while, way into 2024. Before working out what the land might be worth, the pair had to figure out the Section 106 cost and how many affordable homes the council would want. These had to be sold at a 50% discount to a housing association or the council. Turned out 450 'affordable' homes and a Section 106 contribution of £40 million would suffice. George fiddled away on his spreadsheets, altering the number every time Neil came up with new information, or he needed to update the construction and funding costs. Finally, George had a mix he thought might get through planning. This included selling plots for fifty retirement units and 200 private rented sector flats to others. When the sums were done, George was left with a residual £16 million to pay for the land.

Land value appraisal: 1,500 units at Bailey Park

	Average	Units	Total – £ millions	
Income				
Private	£328,000	800	262	
PRS and retirement	£216,000	250	54	
Affordable	£166,000	450	74	
Price uplifts net			35	
Gross development value				425
Residual land value				16
Expenditure				
Section 106	£26,666	1,500	40	
Construction	£155,333	1,500	233	
Professional fees	£8,000	1,500	12	
Marketing	£6,667	1,500	10	
Sales	£3,333	1,500	5	
Finance costs	£24,667	1,500	37	337
Built-in profit				
800 private units	£67,500	800	54	
Rental and retirement	£40,000	250	10	
Affordable units	£8,889	450	4	72
Build cost + profit + residual land value = GDV				425

Bailey Park: the mix

Type	Sale	Rent/retire	Affordable	Total
One-bed flat	17	62	45	124
Two-bed flat	25	105	63	193
Three-bed flat		21		21
Two-bed house	100	62	191	353
Three-bed house	462		135	597
Four-bed detached	154		16	170
Five-bed detached	42			42
Totals	800	250	450	1,500

Flying nook's nest

George's ducks were all in a row when he resigned from Nook in early 2025. By then the farmer, Giles Brown, was on his uppers. Subsidies had shrivelled. Half the land was fallow, the only real earner, a monthly boot fair. The rest was given over to 'horseyculture', grazing and low jumps for ponies. An option to buy the farm had been brokered by Neil. George handed in his resignation to Nook the day he paid Brown £160,000 for the option. Brown would get 50% of the residual land value, minus how much it cost Nook to get planning. That was the deal. Brown could have got a bigger split. But he was frankly desperate to go. The farmer flew to Antigua with his younger lover, bought a beach bar and awaited his further windfall. He had to wait a while.

George set up the Bailey Park Limited Liability Partnership with an initial £250,000 loan secured on George's house. The LLP needed to raise £4 million to pay for costs incurred between applying for permission until selling the first homes. Architects, engineers and planners would now have to be employed. He also needed to raise the £8 million due to Giles Brown if the £16 million land value turned out as forecast.

On the credit side, stood the land. George was popular, well respected. His vision for Bailey Park attracted like-minded investors. George showed them the numbers he had been working on with Neil for nearly two years. He sold 40% of his equity in the LLP for £10 million to a group of High Net Worth investors. The other £2 million came from a loan, attached to the deeds of his two homes.

2025–30

The five years between buying the land and selling the first houses were a trial. George's patience snapped in 2026, at a meeting of sceptical councillors. They could not imagine why George would want to put fewer homes on the land than their rules allowed. They were under pressure from Whitehall to deliver their housing targets. 'I can do this because I'm paying £16 million for the land,' said George. 'If you want to cram 2,000 units on the site, go ahead! Do you know what happens? The landowner will pocket over £40 million instead of £16 million! You want that?' he almost shouted. 'Is cramming official policy? Sod the inhabitants, think of the number of units! Do I want that? No! I want to build decent-sized homes. To build a mixed and stable community. That's what you want, isn't it? We can do this.' They looked at him in wonderment, never having had such candour from a developer. It still took two years to get permission.

Sense of community

George had been in housebuilding for many years and he knew that he needed to keep the local community on side. As time had gone on and he had become more experienced, and more comfortable in his skin, he had begun to realise that if he listened to residents then he stood to benefit. He could learn valuable things from the neighbours. And they needed to be treated with respect, as woe betide any developer who rides roughshod over the local community. The last thing he needed were residents turning up to object to his scheme at the planning committee.

Over his years at Nook Homes George had worked with several people who had been deployed to 'manage the community relations' on various of Sir Ron's schemes. These were PR companies in the main, and George took rather a dim view of their activities. In private, he thought they were just cynical consultants on the make. In public he expressed the view that his own company would not subcontract this work, believing it to be too important to be entrusted to third parties. It was his company and he would forge a relationship with his community.

Violet's teapot

But he couldn't do everything himself. One of the first appointments George made at Bailey Park was Violet Marsh, a striking lady in early middle age, who managed all of George's stakeholder engagement. This wasn't restricted merely to the Parish Council and residents' associations but ranged through dealing with groups such as the local scouts, football clubs, mother and toddler groups, as well as liaising with all the local schools and setting up an apprenticeships scheme for construction operatives at the local FE College.

Violet proved to be worth her weight in gold. She was fond of saying that 'the experts in any place are the people who live there' and she later became legendary at Bailey Park, always available for a cup of tea with anyone. After the local newspaper had run a human-interest story, Violet had become rather famous for owning the biggest teapot anyone had ever seen. This painstaking work with the community stood George in good stead as he went into the local authority to negotiate his planning permission. Violet Marsh became indispensable again, as she assisted new residents at Bailey Park to settle in, once again wielding that teapot, and energetically introducing newbies to the local amenities and like-minded neighbours.

Planning permission

Getting planning permission was only half the battle. The council had managed to postpone involvement in the new planning regime which gave automatic outline permission to developers of large schemes on land like George's, which was going to be zoned as 'growth land' once the council buckled under to Whitehall imposed targets. Meanwhile, George had to operate under the old regime – and that included opening his spreadsheets to scrutiny by the council and their paid advisors. Done to negotiate Planning Obligations, more commonly known as 'Section 106' agreements, named after a clause in the 1990 Town and Country Planning Act. George found the 'you pay us, we give you planning' pretty distasteful. The new rules would have made it much easier. Just one 'Infrastructure Tax' based on a set of tables supplied by government and only payable when the homes were sold or let.

His Section 106 contribution was £40 million, largely for a school and community centre. But it did include £2,000 for the upkeep of the council crematorium. Folks would die as well as live on Bailey Park was the justification.

Permission was finally granted in early 2027. That was the point at which George had to settle his debt with the farmer, who, by then, had hired a professional advisor. A final appraisal was done. George was then able to raise a £100 million development loan. Happily, swings and roundabouts brought the land residual land value back to £16 million. After some negotiation with Giles Brown's land agent, the deal was done. Brown was given half the £12 million left in the pot after £4 million of costs were deducted. His £6 million was wired into an offshore account in Antigua. Done on the advice of his new tax advisor.

But ground was not broken for nearly another year. Access turned into a nightmare. A builder owned a verge through which site access was needed. They had retained ownership of the strip after their plans for homes on George's land were abandoned years before. 'Quite a common occurrence, apparently,' said Neil, but the lawyers had failed to spot the issue. The builder wanted a slice of George's development profits. He was being held to ransom.

Ransom stripped

George knew there was something of a dog-eat-dog culture in respect of what is termed, among the aficionados, 'ransom' strips. Retained strips of land on the edges of developments held in case someone bought the next field. Or keeping ownership of a thin strip on the undeveloped side of an access road. If another developer had to cross the strip to gain access to their land, woe betide. The owner of the strip can demand 33% of the increase in the value of the land if the owner gets planning permission. Huge sums of money, for doing nothing more than saying 'stand and deliver'.

A subset of specialist lawyers skilled in 'ransom strip' wrangles thrived in this unproductive sector. Most real estate consultancies had a 'service line' dealing in ransom strip disputes. Lucrative fees were earned by either acting as second to the gun-toting owner of the strip or defending a victim from a serious financial wound. Activity excused as part of the cut and thrust of the development world. As if being held up at gunpoint and robbed of your valuables, is the risk you take driving down a country lane.

Those who prosper in this rough trade have to thank a dispute (Stokes vs Cambridge) way back in 1961 between a developer who wanted to build sheds on twelve acres of land and a council which owned under one acre of land, which needed to be crossed. Cambridge council squeezed an extra £10,411 on top of the £2,250 the land was worth. A sum calculated as being one-third of the land value of the site with permission for sheds. A percentage which has set the precedent for countless subsequent fights.

George knew haggling can delay development or halt it completely by making land unviable. Some strips are caused by an accident or a quirk. Others are because the local authority concerned has not paid due attention to where exactly a road is to be situated along the edge of a site and the applicant on that land has left a margin – whether this was on purpose or by accident.

After he bought Bailey Park and discovered that he was going to be held to ransom, he appealed to the owner's decency. Back came the tart response: 'Land ownership and planning regulation in the UK go back many years and the registering of parcels and strips of land to enable value has simply been part and parcel of everyday commercial activity throughout the industry over many decades. Sometimes it works in our favour and at other times against.'

George then asked the development manager of a strategic land business how he coped. 'They happen all the time. I've got three currently in dispute. Two in our favour and one against. They are a complete pain. But you have to live with it.' A settlement was finally reached. It cost George £5 million from his £8 million contingency sum; a third went to lawyers. By late summer of 2028, the entrance slips and spine road for the whole site were in and finished. Work began on the show homes. By 2030, George's £100 million loan had drained down to £20 million. Thankfully 150 homes were up and had started to sell.

Prefabrication

George wanted to prefabricate as much as possible, but he was wary. Homes built of steel in the 1950s had rusted. Towers made of concrete panels in the 1960s had collapsed. Around the time he was born, timber frame houses were being used on 25% of all new homes in the UK. A few fires in 1983, followed by an inflammatory TV documentary from *World in Action* and – crash – within a year timber frame's market share collapsed. George worried that some gimcrack system would fail, end up on TV and scare buyers off his houses. But, by 2030 prefabrication was far cheaper than building on site. The risk had to be taken.

SPOW

Another of George's concerns was the speed at which to sell the private units. Nook used price adjustments to regulate sales to between 0.60 and 0.80 homes per week, per site. The Sales per Outlet per Week (SPOW) of thirty to forty a year governed the output of half a dozen volume housebuilders. When George joined Nook from college, he went on a high-flyer's induction course. His degree in development had left him with the impression that 'if only the planning system was made more efficient' Britain could build many more homes.'How the planning system can deliver more homes' was indeed George's thesis.

The course took place at a hotel in Buxted, East Sussex. The smell from the local chicken-processing plant hung in the air. George recycled his dissertation in front of Sir Ron Pinchup, who sat, arms folded, saying nothing. Later that week Sir Ron called him in for 'a little chat'.'You're a bright lad, George.' Ron smiled.'But forget all that planning bollocks. If it was easy to get permission, we'd have more competition. We have to tell Whitehall their system needs fixing, otherwise they'd say, why can't you hit our targets? We're here to make a profit, son. Back in 2007, our rivals forgot that. Some sucked the political Kool-Aid. Over-extended. Then came the crash. Where was all that so-called demand then? Evaporated. Gone. Nearly killed off two of our rivals. Both survived, more's the pity.'

A proper balance

'Now, we talk to each other and agree on a proper balance. Stick to selling under one a week; makes sound business sense. We can all make decent margins without straining resources. We keep risk to a minimum. You never know when the demand will evaporate. Course, we could build more. But we look after shareholders, not the government.' Nook regularly made profits of 20%. 'Why would you sell more?' asked Sir Ron rhetorically. 'Because the latest housing minister wants to please their annual conference with a target!' Sir Ron became a billionaire while continuing to attack planners.

When he handed in his resignation at Nook, Sir Ron was kind enough to George to host his farewell dinner. They joked over a story in the paper that day from the umpteenth minister of the twenty-first century promising to build more homes. 'What's 'e going to use?' Sir Ron laughed. 'A f****** magic trowel!' Every time George smelled fried chicken, he remembered SPOW. When demand fell at Nook, more houses were released for sale and discounts quietly introduced. When demand rose, fewer houses were released at higher prices. All done to keep the SPOW valve set at producing under one a week.

Selling forty units a year, it would take twenty years to sell all 800 private units. A snails-pace way to build a community. Bailey Park therefore *had* to beat the competition on both value and size to sell more quickly. *Bailey Park had to be finished by 2040 at the latest*, thought George. *All 800 sold.* Not least because that was the timeframe used in the appraisal. A deal was done with Swedish builder, Bygga, which had come to the UK in 2020 and spent about £30 million erecting a pre-fab factory in Gwent. By 2030, there were far too many of these prefabrication sheds. George was able to negotiate knock-down terms. Bygga badly needed the order. They agreed to take on the £65 million civil contract to build the roads and services. Bygga also negotiated three separate contracts to build the public and private rental and the retirement units. If sales slowed, the Swedes could fall back on these contracts to keep the workforce busy.

Non-private sales

George had long been negotiating to divest the 700 affordable, private and retirement units. The deal with Sunblest Retirement for fifty flats was a doozy. Easily done with a business that had waxed into a huge business after catching the tail of the baby-boomer generation. All they wanted was a serviced plot of land near the shops. Done. After some dancing around, George chose Homes for People as the provider for the 450 affordable homes. Some would be rented out permanently. Others sold in slices to tenants who waited long enough. George settled on insurance giant Life & Homes to supply the 200 flats close to the centre of Bailey Park that would be rented privately in perpetuity.

George wanted Bailey Park to be 'tenure blind' – with the private and 'affordable' rented units pepper-potted sensitively throughout the community. He'd seen too many examples at Nook where the 'affordable' homes were tucked shamefully away and private rented blocks filled with noisy young transients next to retirement homes. Negotiations with Life & Homes and Homes for People lasted for almost two years. Both had very different visions from George, who lost his temper during one early meeting with Homes for People. He asked if they would like to give more space to their tenants.

The development director's reply boiled down to, 'We can't possibly build our houses 25% bigger. Ruins our business model.'

'Have you any idea of how much you are already leeching out of the system?' retorted George to a woman he knew earned ten times the average wage. 'You are getting £150 million of homes half price and you can't make them a bit bigger!' he shouted. 'A subsidy that has dragged the residual land value down by £75 million. A subsidy from the landowner to the state.' This was not the best argument to use against a state-supported body. But he was angry. *Everyone deserves better*, thought George.

Ease of management

Homes for People insisted all their units must be in one place – for ease of management. They were perfectly happy to take the worst locations; in fact, they rather expected it. Life & Homes had similar demands, to build flats to their sizes and specifications – and all in the same place. Except, for them, the best places were near the shops. George knew Bailey Park would be blighted in the eyes of private buyers. They would see housing association blocks filled with those... well, not quite their sort of people – and those in the private flats as transients. But George was forced to comply. Plot sales to these guys would kick start Bailey Park. He allowed Homes & Life their 200 private rentals close to, and in some cases over the shops, reasoning it would allow him to start work early on the central plaza. Homes for People got to group their 450 affordable homes out by the ring road after George secured a promise that both would start on site in 2030.

2030–40

Bygga began work on the roads and sewers in 2028. The Swede's were on contract to build two private homes a week starting in March 2029, with the caveat that if sales fell below one a week after the first 150, they would slow down. Those 150 were up – and mostly sold by late 2030. Word had begun to spread – the homes on Bailey Park were better than your average new homes. Bygga began working for Homes for People and Life & Homes.

By 2033, George was flying: 300 private homes and flats sold, £100 million banked and the LLP cashflow went positive for the first time. Money was coming in from plot sales from Homes for Life and Homes for People. The £37 million budgeted for interest payments on the development loan looked safe. The school opened that year. The shops and community centre were finished. The rented and 'affordable' flats were 65% built and occupied. Then came the mid-thirties crash. Bang. Demand dwindled. For two years he sold one a week, a hundred in total. Bygga was not happy. Luckily, they had the remaining units for Homes for People and Life & Homes to finish. Thankfully the market recovered in 2035 and over the next five years, George sold the remaining 300 private units at a good clip of two per week. More than double the rate of nearby sites. Thanks to the size and generous spacing of his homes, George was also able to charge more.

Did George make money?

George was fifty-five when the last house was sold in Bailey Park at the end of 2039. He was thinking of retiring and could afford to do so. Bailey Park had been half a life's work, but work well rewarded. Did George make the £72 million profit on the £425 millions of income guessed at in the development appraisal back in 2025? These guesses never quite work out in reality. Costs rose more than anticipated. The mid-thirties slump hit hard. But house prices rose more than anticipated, especially after the rail services improved in 2035. George ended up making £60 million gross, for himself and his investors. Gross being the word. Bailey Park LLP was the company George set up in 2025. Fairies did not manage this fifteen-year development. A five-strong team working for George did. Each year for fifteen years the LLP incurred costs. George, plus an administrator, and three people to manage the planning, construction and sales, cost £10 million. That left £50 million to be distributed among shareholders, money distributed in various-sized lumps over the final ten years of the project. Those who backed George in return for 40% of the equity were repaid handsomely: £20 million for an investment of £10 million. Another £5 million went to Neil Grabbier, leaving George £25 million. What did George do with his dividends? Bought more land, of course. But that's another story.

Development exemplar

By 2040, Bailey Park had achieved academic celebrity, at least among master-planners. Groups of students could be seen measuring the width of the streets and taking pictures of people's small front gardens and drives and peering into the bigger back gardens, noting down how little 'soft' communal space was left for the council to maintain. They surmised this was because estates where councils were in charge, verges and hedges tended to be unkempt. They observed how the three parks were well-tended, concluding this was because they were popular with young and old voters alike.

Bailey Park even became a financial appraisal study for students studying land economy at Cambridge. What conclusions did students reach in their dissertations? Nothing too surprising. The costs of building fewer, bigger homes were balanced by the higher prices and rents that could be charged. The real gains were those of permanent 'social value'. What might be called 'community gains'. Occupants stayed longer, leading to a more stable community. The crime rate was lower, employment higher. The social mix meant that Bailey Park was neither blessed – nor cursed – as being seen as too posh or too working class. What did Ryan and Lulu thing of this? Nothing. They just knew they had found a nice place to live.

TWO

POTTER'S FIELD

'Some see things the way they are and ask why?'
George Bernard Shaw

Part one: Ryan and Lulu

The Ghost family moved to Potter's Field in 2030. The Nook Homes brochure said the name came from some ancient clay workings, found on the land, filled with shards of old pots. Lulu and Ryan had been told there would be a fair number of rented flats. The saleswoman reassured them this was deliberate as 'we are building a mixed, vibrant community'. Explaining the social mix would prevent Potter's Field becoming 'one of those bland 1980s estates'. Lulu and Ryan approved. 'We don't want to live somewhere boring,' they later remembered saying.

Ryan and Lulu were both earning, so able to afford a house in Pinchup Close for £300,000. Just a few hundred of the 2,000 homes planned on the eastern outskirts of Bedford had been built. An unbroken row of narrow three-storey terraces ran up either side of the Close. Each set one or two metres back from the tight curving road. Three-storey semis enclosed the bulb-shaped end of the Close. Ryan and Lulu bought a semi at the top of the bulb. The garden was a bit bigger than most, the high fences fanning back eight metres from the house. Those in the terraces were lucky to get a five-metre garden. The house felt big enough for their needs. No kids, yet. But they wanted three bedrooms, even if the master was a long climb to the second floor. This was going to be their nest.

Lulu's parents were a bit sniffy, remarking on the twelve-foot-wide living room and absence of a dining room. They urged them to buy a bigger place on a 1980s estate on the other side of Bedford. But 'Aid to Own' – a pension fund successor to Help to Buy – was not available on second-hand homes. The offer of a £60,000 loan from a pension fund in return for 20% of the equity clinched it for Ryan and Lulu. It meant they could afford a semi rather than a terrace. The price felt a bit high. But No 29 was new, there was no chain and it smelled nice.

Pinchup close

The couple moved in during the summer. Their new neighbours tended to be in their early thirties, most having been together for a few years – some married, some not. Some had owned flats. Most were ex-renters. One or two had small babies. They were mostly two-income couples. Those living alone tended to be older – divorcees, perhaps? Sociologists would describe the mix as C1/C2. Many commuted to London. Lulu drove to the station and caught the train to her HR job in the City. Ryan worked as 'the tech-guy' at a distribution shed near Junction 13 on the M1. He used a motorbike to get to work, on the days he didn't work from home.

A mild pioneering spirit developed. Barbecues were held in the small back yards, the odd party inside. Gatherings could get a bit cramped if you invited more than three couples. Ryan and Lulu made friends with a couple a few doors away. Raj was a self-employed carpenter, his wife, Karen, a travelling hairdresser. They were trying for a baby. Lulu said she was thinking of having one as well.

Trouble begins

By summer 2031, all forty houses in Pinchup Close were occupied. Five houses had garages and a drive with space to park one car. If they had a second car it was parked on the road outside, as the garages were a bit small for cars and quickly filled up with *stuff*. Those without garages had allotted spots in the mini-car park, reached through an archway on to hard standings, where gardens would normally lie. Most just stuck the car outside the house if there was room. Ryan had been parking his motorbike in a quiet corner, allowing Lulu to use their space for her car. One day a giant four-by-four appeared, usurping Ryan's squatters' rights. This forced Ryan to move his bike into their own spot, making it tricky for Lulu to park. Why did people buy these bloody great cars? One night the pair had a poisonous row, which began with Ryan making a crack about Lulu's driving skills.

Raj was also getting on their nerves, roaring off at dawn in his purple Transit or letting the wretched van block their sunlight when he had no work. His wife Karen had nowhere to park her small Fiat. Visitor spaces began to be fought over by residents when all the homes became occupied. Karen began to squeeze her car onto a verge. Tensions would rise on weekday evenings as the road jammed up like a seaside car park on Bank Holiday Monday. There was an incident when an ambulance had been called to No 25 one day during the summer holidays, when a visiting child had suffered an anaphylactic shock, needing urgent medical attention. The ambulance hadn't been able to get through, and the paramedics had had to stretcher the kid the length of Pinchup Close. Fortunately, the child had not died.

This incident had been reported to the local authority with a joint request from the emergency services, signed by the local police, fire and ambulance leaders, calling for urgent action on controlling the parking. The local authority couldn't (or wouldn't, it being a marginal council seat) do anything. And the senior officer responsible sent a formal acknowledgement and then allowed this letter to slide into his SABU (Self-Adjusting Balls-Ups) tray, taking the view that the emergency services 'merely wished to establish a paper trail' should there be any further incident. Nothing was done. Goodness knows what would have happened had there been a fire.

No more hellos

Neighbourly relations began to cool. Residents stopped saying hello as they walked past each other down the middle of the road, the only place people could pass without brushing shoulders. Owners got into the habit of plugging in their cars by draping charging wires out of their front window at night. Cheaper than using charging stations. One evening an old lady visiting her daughter tripped over a wire and broke her hip. Police were called to prevent a fight. Friends became enemies. Couples blamed each other. Ryan began to feel a need to get out of the Close on the days he worked at home. He began to walk to a pub up on the old main road.

One day he met Karen. She blamed the tension in the Close for not being able to conceive. Ryan said the doctor had put Lulu on pills to calm her, confiding their marriage was in a bit of a mess. Karen confessed Raj was becoming unreasonable. Ryan and Karen became close. In 2033, Ryan and Lulu divorced. When the semi in Pinchup Close was sold, they only got £260,000. Nobody warned them that new homes lose up to 20% of their value when you walk in the door. That fact caused one final blazing blame-game row.

Part two: Sir Ron Pinchup

Potter's Field stands on 100 flat hectares, bought by Nook Homes for £43 million in 2025. Three years earlier, local surveyor Neil Grabbier had sensed which way the wind was blowing. Tales of reviving an old rail link between Oxford and Cambridge were floating around. A new station within five miles of the site was mentioned. Stories about building thousands of homes along a 'Varsity Line' were appearing. In 2020, the government promised five new towns.

Neil Grabbier ran a one-man surveying consultancy in Bedford. He was a Rotary man, a good egg, known to all. He was also a member of the Woburn Golf club, a thirty-six-hole course on the other side of the M1. One day in the summer of 2022, he paired with Giles Brown, a farmer, who mentioned on the 17th he was selling his 100-hectare farm on the outskirts of Bedford. He joked about no longer wanting to rise at dawn to pick cabbages and grub up sugar beet.

Giles said he was days away from taking £2 million from some agent in London. 'He said his clients are long-term holders of agricultural land who preferred to remain anonymous.' Neil gulped and hooked his drive into the pine trees. 'I think I can do better.' The pair cut the 18th hole, hurrying to the clubhouse. Neil confided there was a chance the agent may be fronting for housebuilders or land dealers. They might be looking to buy his fields before anyone caught on that permission for houses might be possible. He suggested Giles put them on hold for a few months.

Neil explained that he might be able to persuade a volume housebuilder to take an option. 'They pay you, say, £50,000 upfront, non-returnable. You agree to give them a few years to get permission. Then you agree on a price for the land, based on a proportion of what's called the residual land value, minus the cost of getting permission. Don't worry about that now. What I can tell you is that it will be higher than the current offer. You give me a 10% commission on the option and 1% on the price. Deal?'

'Deal!' said Giles.

Approaching builders

Neil began to approach housebuilders in the spring of 2023. But only after doing his homework on what mix of homes might get planning permission. The parcel was too big for all but the biggest housebuilders. Number one, Holland Homes didn't want to know. Number two, Tinker McDonald, were already building nearby and said no. Number three, Aldertree suggested £25 million – with more hedges than a maze. *If the ground turned out to be unsuitable… if services to the site cost more than A… if they had to pay more than B in contributions to the council… if the number of affordable units exceeded C… if the 'affordable discount' was more than D... If we get out of bed the wrong side*, thought Neil, who stopped answering their emails.

Then a 'strategic land' company expressed interest. Their model: get permission, put in the services and flog off plots to smallish housebuilders. Neil sensed this 'strat-land' player wanted to cut him out. So, he cut them out. He then worked up a plan that might appeal to Nook Homes, Britain's fourth-biggest housebuilder. Founder Sir Ron Pinchup wanted to be *Numero Uno*. A chase for sales had depleted his land bank, down to two years' supply by the time Neil pitched his plan in late 2023. 'Get permission for 2,000 units, put in the roads and services. Flog a chunk of plots to the private rented guys.'

Sir Ron said no, at first, after doing a back-of-the-fag-packet calculation. 'It will cost me over £40 million to buy the land, same again in 106 payments, same again to service the plots before I start building. Maybe £120 million out before a unit is sold.'

'Doesn't have to be that way,' argued Neil. 'You will risk a few million to get planning. You could make a killing selling plots into the private rented sector. The farmer is happy to take staged payments. A one-year tax bill would kill him.'

'OK,' said Sir Ron, with seeming reluctance, 'go ahead, work up some numbers with my guys.' Neil sensed Sir Ron was keen to top up Nook's land bank.

Nook history

Nook Homes was Britain's fourth-largest housebuilder by 2023, selling 10,000 units a year, half the number of Holland Homes. Sir Ron Pinchup was then in his mid-sixties. The former carpenter ran the business he founded in 1985 with great attention to detail. The 'K' came from giving millions to support a royal charity that gave working-class kids a chance in life. Sir Ron liked to arrive unannounced on sites at 7.00 am in his black chauffeur-driven Range Rover, then drag the hapless site manager across the site, pointing out poor workmanship. He didn't need to be doing this. By then, Sir Ron was taking out about £4 million a year in pay and bonuses. A long-term incentive scheme based on the rise in Nook's share price gifted him £35 million in 2022. Sir Ron had sold down his stake in Nook to 15% by 2025. Even then, he hardly knew what to do with his dividends on top of the cash piling up. He was worth about £300 million. But he liked money. He liked going to work.

Sir Ron's attention to site-level detail meant the company had a solid reputation. Nook had ten regional offices and employed more than 1,000 staff. The day-to-day running of the company had been handed to 'Delivery Dave', as everyone called the trained accountant who had joined Sir Ron from a utility company in 2009: the year of Nook's 'anus non-horribilis', as Sir Ron liked to mispronounce it. Sir Ron had always remembered the earlier 1990 crash; it nearly finished his tiny company off. Imprinted on his mind was a site in Somerset. Nook had bought land enough for 500 units on the outskirts of a market town in the late 1980s. The site was bounded by a canal on one side. The only way he could get permission was to build what amounted to one quadrant of a ring road around the town and bridge over the canal – before he could sell a single unit. He agreed. There was a crash. Millions lost. It was years before he recovered the money.

When the market stopped dead in 2009, Sir Ron had not over-extended, unlike his bigger rivals. Nook was selling 6,000 units a year in 2008. The next twelve months were pretty horrible. Completions crashed to 4,500 even as discounts of up to 15% were offered on top of hidden incentives such as free kitchen upgrades. Land purchases were suspended, regional offices closed, with 300 staff made redundant. Construction work was halted. There was a housing crisis; not the one the government was always bleating on about. The crisis was that nobody wanted to buy. Even so, Nook scraped profit that year of £11 million on sales of £700 million.

Three--year plan

Nook's three-year business plans were founded upon caution. Sir Ron's rules were these: never let construction get too far ahead of sales; if you are selling quickly, prices are too low – put them up; if you are not selling, stop building. Not hard rules to follow. Sir Ron found that adjusting prices to keep sales ticking over at just under one a week per site allowed him to expand at about 10% per year and earn profits of 20% without undue risk. Most of his rivals did the same and all flourished. Some more than others. By 2020, three of those hardest-hit in 2009 had stretched away from Nook. 'Come on, Ron.' They would laugh over the roast duck at their regular 'Top Ten' dinners at the Intercontinental on Park Lane. 'You are losing your bottle!' This irked him more than they imagined.

Nook's land bank had shrunk to 19,000 units by 2022, less than two years' supply. That – and the ribbing he had to take from rivals – tipped Sir Ron toward buying from Farmer Giles. In early 2024, Nook's board finally agreed to option the land – but only based on Nook doing no more than the 700 units. The council would want 500 'affordable' units. That left 800 plots for the Private Rented Sector and retirement (PRS) guys. Nook paid Brown £50,000 for a ten-year option, with a five-year extension if both agreed. The price of the land would only be agreed after Nook had got planning and nailed down costs.

There was a pond at the lowest end of the site. Sir Ron had a tank of newt-eating carp illegally poured into the water in the dead of the night as soon as the option was signed, thereby making sure that there was no threat from having to protect great crested newts, which could have both caused delays and proved expensive.

Potter's Field: the mix

Type	Sale	Rent/retire	Affordable	Total
One-bed flat		250	150	400
Two-bed flat		200	200	400
Three-bed flat			50	50
Two-bed house	100	250	50	400
Three-bed house	500	100	50	650
Four-bed detached	100			100
Totals	700	800	500	2,000

Masterplan

Nook's consultants took eighteen months to draw up a masterplan and pull together the application. The council had successfully staved off plans by government to introduce automatic outline permission on land zoned for 'growth.' Crammer + Partners, a pliable firm of architects who worked regularly for Nook drew up the plans. Only seventy out of the 100 hectares could take houses; the rest was needed for the spine road, village centre and school. Getting 2,000 homes on seventy hectares squeezed the density up to nearly twenty-nine per hectare. But they pushed, as Sir Ron had told them 2,000 was in the appraisal.

The documentation needed to support a major application could fill a small skip. There were dozens of tree-filled drawings from Crammer, a 400-page environmental impact statement from Greenwash Consultants. Carefully 'curated' results of a public consultation carried out by Silent Persuaders, Nook's PR consultants, were provided. But the most valuable document was drawn up by Nook's planning consultants, A–Z Planners, led by the redoubtable Clive Geikie. A–Z knew the ever-morphing planning rules forwards, backwards – and from Whitehall down to Parish council. Their 200-page justification was a hard-to-challenge masterpiece.

Nook had racked up fees of close to £5 million by the time copies of the application were uploaded to the planning portal and hard copies delivered by a lorry in early 2027. The opposition had been organised well before the plans were published on the council website. Obligatory consultations with local groups meant the anti-development lobby was prepared. Attacks were coordinated by councillors representing wards closest to the land. They threw everything at Nook: 'The houses are too small. There is not enough parking. There will be traffic congestion. There are not enough affordable units. The crime rate will rise!'

'Relax,' said A–Z. 'All the usual non-salient objections from all the usual suspects. We have sought assurances from those who count: Highways England, the Environment Agency, Heritage England, the Internal Drainage Board and Network Rail.' As A–Z said, these 'statutory consultees' had the power to stop an application in its tracks if they felt the development would cause too much traffic, be bad for the planet, cause flooding, or be built over ancient ruins or simply clog up the trains. Local folk were to be feared far less.

Permission was granted by the end of 2027. Pretty quick for such a big site. Nook had A-team consultants. There was one low point when Nook's lawyers, Snarler & Sons, had to remind councillors of the penalties for refusing planning. The council can't just say no because it feels like it. Nook would appeal. The costs of an appeal could run into millions. If the council lost, the ratepayers footed the bill. As long as the planning application fell within a set of well-defined guidelines, the council dare not refuse. A–Z had been well paid to make very sure that the application was refusal-proof.

Section 106

A–Z had entered into parallel negotiations with the council, which had successfully staved off government plans to introduce an infrastructure levy. A tax set by government and only payable once the homes were sold. So, Nook still had to open their books, declare anticipated costs, admit profit margins, anticipate income and show what they could pay for the land. The grounds for argument were far and wide. Happily, A–Z could draw on their experience from far and wide. The council could not. So, they hired rival planning consultant, 123 Partners. The principals knew each other of old. Fred Groom of 123 once worked alongside Clive Geikie.

Fred took three of A–Z's best planners with him when he left to set up his own consultancy during the golden years for Section 106 negotiations a decade earlier. Fred could argue how many angels can you get on a brickbat with the best of them. Nook began by saying they could afford no more than £15,000 per unit. But Fred jacked them up £20,000 – £40 million for the 2,000 units. An extra £10 million, so Fred earned his corn. Potter's Field would get a primary school, a small park, a community centre and a doctor's surgery. Everyone shook hands after months of haggling. Fred and Clive knew to keep it friendly. They would no doubt come across each other again.

The final of about twenty appraisals estimated the residual land value to be £43 million. The numbers threw up £81 million profit on an income of £500 million. Not bad. A 16% margin on sales. A bit low for Sir Ron's liking.

Land value appraisal: 2,000 units at Potter's Field

Income	Average	Units	Total – £ millions	
Private	£300,000	700	210	
PRS and retirement	£220,000	800	176	
Affordable	£150,000	500	75	
Price uplifts net			39	
Gross development value				500
Residual land value				43
Expenditure				
Section 106	£20,000	2,000	40	
Construction	£123,000	2,000	246	
Professional fees	£9,000	2,000	18	
Marketing	£6,000	2,000	12	
Sales	£3,759	2,000	7	
Finance costs	£26,500	2,000	53	376
Built-in profit				
Private	£60,000	700	42	
Rental and retirement	£42,400	800	34	
Affordable	£10,000	500	5	81
Build cost + profit + residual land value = GDV				500

Deal done

With permission granted and costs more or less nailed down, it was time to do a deal with Giles Brown. The site was valued using rules in an enormously thick 'Red Book' published by the Royal Institution of Chartered Surveyors, used by all valuers. The Gross Development Value was £500 million, the costs £376 million and the allowable profit £81 million. The residual land value was, therefore, £43 million. All guesses, of course. After spirited arguments lasting several months, Neil agreed his client would take 80% of the residual land value, minus £5 million in planning costs. Giles Brown walked straight to his tax advisors clutching a banker's draft for just under £30 million.

In early 2028, three deals were signed. One with Sunblest Homes for 200 retirement units. A second for 600 PRS flats with Brown Stone, a giant US rental business. The deal for the 500 affordable homes was done with Homes for People, a housing association with philanthropic roots, but now steeped in commercial acid. They bargained harder than the Yanks. Nook agreed to build all the roads and services, essentially providing their partners with serviced plots they would pay for upon delivery.

On to site

All Nook homes were internally designated by the number of bedrooms/ sizes in square feet. The 1/380 Studio, the 1/450 Nook and the 2/650 Double-Nook were stacked into blocks up to six storeys high. There were four variants of houses: the 3/750 Snug Terrace, the 3/850 Snug Semi and the 3/950 Snug Detached. For posher sites, a 4/1100 Super-Snug was available. The priority for Nook was the show area. Nook's flags for Potter's Field were fluttering over a selection of units by June 2029. A 3/950 detached and a pair of 3/850 three-storey semis were erected, surrounded by turfed lawns and crunchy white gravel. Tea and fresh cakes were always on tap in the main show home. A mini-marketing push saw fifty pre-sold by Christmas.

Prefabrication

All of Nook's homes were factory-built. The insides, that is; a brick shell and tiled roof were always used. Sir Ron was wary of 'Murphy's law' – 'what can go wrong will go wrong'. Some housebuilders were using 'clip-on' outside walls, brick 'slips' glued to panels. Some companies were prefabricating roofs that looked like they were covered in clay tiles but were actually pressed from thin steel, pitched at an uncommonly low angle of 22.5 degrees, an angle determined by the height of railway bridges on the route out of the factory to building sites. But these sorts of houses were only sold to cash-strapped housing associations and councils. Those who could not afford to buy, or rent on the private market, got what they got for a cheap rent – and were hardly going to complain.

Completion

Nook's four-inch brick walls and 45% pitched roofs radiated assurance, tradition, solidity. The porch, the panelled front door, the brass furniture were all designed for 'kerb-appeal'. The show house interiors were dressed with care. Nook's marketing team was the best in the business. Fortunes were spent researching the tastes of the target market. Great thought also went into the selection of smaller-than-average furniture and the placing of more than the average number of mirrors.

By late '29 the spine road and services were complete. The homes in Pinchup Close finished. Folk began to move in in the spring of 2030. By 2033, Homes for People had finished three-quarters of their 500 units up by the ring road. This was a run of eight-storey blocks Crammer + Partners felt would help screen the private homes from traffic noise and help maintain prices. Brown Stone had whooshed up 300 of their PRS flats. The '33 recession slowed things. But not so much for the PRS stock, which steadily rented. The rest of the 'affordable' and the remaining PRS units and the retirement flats were up and occupied by 2035.

Nook's bottom lines

Nook sold the final 350 units between 2035 and 2039, a period of moderate price growth driven by the growing prosperity of the area. Back in 2025, £39 million had been added to income on the appraisal. This was what Nook's mighty software had guessed to be the increase in house prices minus the increase in costs over fifteen years. These guesses never work out in reality. Costs rose more than anticipated. But house prices also rose more than anticipated, especially after the rail services improved in 2035. The profit of £81 million anticipated back in 2025 shrunk a touch to £75 million. Barely worth noting.

Half the profits at Potter's Field had come from the 700 private units. A miserly £5 million from the affordable units. Where Nook had done well was to sell 800 plots to Brown Stone and Sunblest, scooping £34 million in profits over the first seven years. But the American smart-mouths from Brown Stone drove Nook's site staff to despair. The whining sanctimony of Homes for People was an added burden. Ron's faithful lieutenant 'Delivery Dave' was in charge by 2040. Sir Ron had stopped visiting Potter's Field in his old age. He found it depressing not being able to attack the scrappy workmanship on the affordable units. Nook never again got involved in sites of more than 500 units.

Legacy

The 'Potter's Field' brand was forgotten within a couple of years of the signboards coming down. No students of design or development visited. Potter's Field became like hundreds of other large settlements across the land. Not that bad. Just not that good. A bit ugly. A bit cramped. Sir Ron recalled that chap George Bailey, who used to work for him, going on about the 'ghosts in the machine', blathering on about the need to give occupants more space inside and out. But without planning laws insisting upon minimum sizes and maximum densities, the housing world continued to turn much as it always had. Who were housebuilders to object? More homes equalled more profit. Two three-floor semis the size of one detached produced more profit. Same went for those building private flats to rent: two one-bed flats of 400 square feet each attracted 30% more rent that a single two-bed flat of 800 square feet. The higher you build, the better. Each additional floor shrank the land price per unit. No good moaning about the way things are. After all, nobody felt it was their duty to make things better.

Back in the real world

In 2018, the government appointed a group of the Great and the Good to discover ways to assuage public disquiet over ugly housing estates. Aesthetes dominated the Building Better, Building Beautiful Commission. Their 'Living with Beauty' report was published in February 2020. The findings are discussed in Chapter Four. Housing Secretary Robert Jenrick then promised to 'embed the principles of good design' in a review of the planning system that will include a model design code that will 'set clear parameters for promoting the design and style of homes and neighbourhoods local people want to see'. These were promises that will 'make tree-lined streets the norm', said Jenrick.

The Ministry of Housing, Communities and Local Government followed up in mid-March 2020 with a pre-cursor to planning reforms in which Jenrick promised to give 'people a stake in society, which means ensuring we are delivering the sorts of homes where people want to raise their children, to grow old together and can be good neighbours'. Jenrick's remarks were informed by a report produced by Right of Centre think tank, Policy Exchange. 'Rethinking the Planning System for the 21st Century' was published in January 2020. Each government has its favourite Think Tank. The author, Jack Airey, was a member of the 'Building Beautiful' Commission and is now a policy advisor in Number 10. Policy Exchange then produced a collection of essays in June 2020, under the title 'Planning Anew'.

Underpinning the 'Beauty' report sits a set of financial foundations, laid by Knight Frank. Figures on the real costs and actual values compiled in a 124-page 'Cost and Value' addendum. Researchers examined cost and sales data on large-scale schemes where 'beauty' was put ahead of utility. The six fully-examined schemes were: Poundbury, Dorset; Fairford Leys, Aylesbury; Oakgrove, Milton Keynes; Newhall, Harlow; Accordia, Cambridge and Coed Darcy in Neath.

Knight Frank does not pretend that the cost of making the homes better than the standard model works everywhere. Nor does it suggest this is an easy path to follow. But the findings were clear:

+ High-quality housing should not erode returns.
+ A value premium of 15% is achievable.
+ Quality sustains pricing for larger dwellings enabling more Gross Development Value per hectare.
+ Value endures in quality development.

BUT

+ Public subsidy is required to deliver community benefits in challenging locations.
+ Delivery is typically constrained by demand, not supply.
+ Blunt supply-side policies risk the unintended consequence of the wrong development in the wrong place.
+ Large projects carry more than their fair share of infrastructure costs, allowing other developments to 'free ride' on value.

Fairford Leys example

'Fairford Leys illustrates housebuilders that believed following a high-quality agenda would erode profitability, but the sales premium they had ignored in fact offset higher costs.' That is the conclusion above from the Knight Frank study of a development of 2,500 homes near Aylesbury, on land owned by the Ernest Cook Trust. John Simpson was the architect of the outline planning application submitted in 1988, which won permission in 1990. A conditional Development Agreement was entered into between the Trust and a consortium of housebuilders in 1993. The consortium included Wimpey, Bryant Homes, Taywood Homes and Admiral Homes. The first house was built and sold in 1997, and the last house was sold in 2008. A pretty historic example. But one which bought a 14.5% 'quality' price premium. Not that the builders believed this would happen. Two charts neatly illustrate the perception gap between volume builders and those who want to build 'better'. The first chart shows a feared drop from £483,000 to £97,000 an acre due to the costs of 'building better.' The second the actual drop – to £430,000.

Fear that quality would depress land values

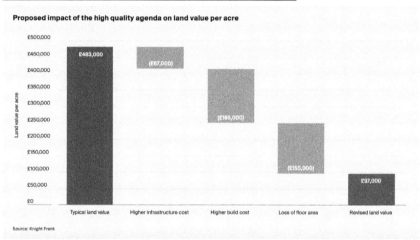

Proposed impact of the high quality agenda on land value per acre

Source: Knight Frank

The reality of what happened by building 'better'

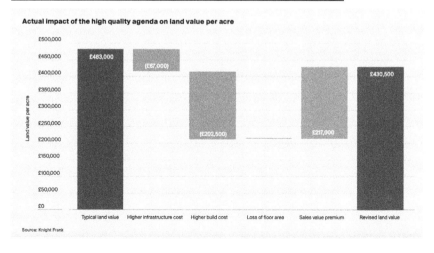

Actual impact of the high quality agenda on land value per acre

Source: Knight Frank

Newhall

Newhall lies east of Harlow. It is a development of approximately 2,900 units. Phase 1 (600 homes) is completed, whilst Phase 2 (2,300 homes) was under construction in early 2020. In total, approximately 1,100 units have been constructed and sold. The summary says it all: 'Newhall illustrates how tensions can arise between two parties – in this case, a landowner and housebuilders – with different time horizons. Newhall has now favoured a longer-term partnership approach to sharing future value with its development partner where both parties should be aligned in a shared goal of building value.' Let Knight Frank tell the tale:

Knight Frank findings

'Newhall is built on land owned by the Soper and Moen family. The project began in 1995. Design and control were of prime importance given the family's previous experience at Church Langley (also developed on family-owned land), where good design was promised but not secured and hence never achieved. The family's ambition was not to allow that to happen a second time around. They were convinced that good design and high-quality materials would lead to better land values, more than offsetting the higher costs involved.

'Newhall Projects Ltd adopted the role of master developer and has sold serviced land parcels to Cala, Barratt, Countryside, Linden and Bellway. They have also sold self-build plots. More recently, they entered into a land leasing arrangement with Countryside Properties, which has paid an upfront fee and a fixed percentage for transfer of freehold plots at the time of dwelling sales. Newhall has promoted contemporary architecture, controlled via a Design Code prepared by Studio Real. The scheme has won several architectural awards.

'The landowner had many challenges enforcing the design code during the delivery stage. All too often the construction *teams on the ground cut corners and failed to deliver what had been contractually committed when the land was purchased. The housebuilders often cited the higher costs of delivering the Newhall design codes and were constantly striving to value engineer the architectural designs and materials. The contractual provisions lacked teeth because the land had been conveyed to the housebuilders, and the landowner's attempts to curate the quality of the housing delivery only served to cause tensions with the housebuilders. The constant pressure from housebuilders inevitably took its toll and led to some compromise.*

'Partly as a reaction to the pressures of dealing with housebuilders the landowner embarked on developing their parcel at Newhall called North Chase. Its timing coincided with the credit crisis of 2007/08 and by 2009 the landowner was under pressure from funders to dispose of unsold units. This caused the landowner to price take and to accept lower offers than they had previously, causing the erosion of the Newhall premium. As time went on, those sales caused lower mortgage valuations which forced buyers to pay less than they had been prepared to. The self-fulfilling nature of mortgage valuations meant that the premium proved challenging to recover once it had been lost.

'Newhall is a project that is at a crossroads. It has now favoured a longer-term partnership with Countryside Properties, which has given the landowner and the housebuilder the same time horizon and each party an equitable share in future value. It is felt that this has the potential to align both parties towards the same goal. Whether it will be successful will be the subject of future reflection.'

Like the fictional George Bailey, the real Soper and Moen families wanted to build bigger better houses. The sales data for those being resold shows an average size of 952 square feet, 15–20% larger than most comparable homes in the area. And was there a sales premium for quality? After a lot of fiddling around to get an exact like-for-like comparison, Knight Frank concluded yes – 12.9%.

Stewardship model

Knight Frank partner Charlie Dugdale is the author of the report. Dugdale also authored an essay on land value capture for the June 2020 Policy Exchange report, 'Planning Anew'. Here Dugdale explains his favoured option, the stewardship model:

> 'The housebuilding sector is a product of the profit motive and how land is sold. Because housebuilders need to pay for the land, they need to obtain a return within a timeframe to satisfy shareholders which incentivises cutting costs. If the land is vested into partnerships as equity within a stewardship model, with both parties sharing in the future value, then both parties are aligned in building long-term value. A stewardship model can refocus the profit motive to long-term value-driven objectives, as opposed to shorter-term cost-driven objectives. How we deliver land engenders the behaviour that follows.

> 'Under the "stewardship" model the land is kept within the freehold ownership of the landowner until homes are sold to occupiers. Development partners perform the development activity under a building lease and share in the future value of sales, or profit emanating from those sales. Because there is no need to fund large land purchases, smaller SME developers can compete with national housebuilders.

> 'Today, private landowners are strongly incentivised to sell land. The main issue is tax. If they sell to a housebuilder, proceeds are treated as Capital Gains Tax and tithed at a maximum of 20%. If they put the land into a "stewardship" model the eventual proceeds are taxed as income – perhaps at 40% or more – double the amount if they sold. We talk to lots of landowners. Many would like to think longer-term but when they see the tax implications the shutters come down. We see this resolved through an "ISA"-style wrapper for landowners seeking to adopt a stewardship role. This would allow income to be treated as though it were a capital gain.

'At the moment much of the public sector hides behind "best consideration" guidance. Our studies show that best consideration can be achieved through longer-term stewardship models. This may be evidence enough to persuade the public sector estate not to sell the family silver. If not, we recommend the evidence should be combined with new guidance from Government telling public sector bodies that the de facto assumption should be that best consideration is achieved through stewardship models. Given a public sector estate worth some £450 billion, this would fundamentally impact the housebuilder model towards delivering lasting value for communities. Also, instead of selling the family silver, the public sector would create more long-term value and income to support public services.'

Fineborough model

Knight Frank produced a second, separate addendum to the 'Living with Beauty' report, called 'Building in Beauty': the story of a typical farming family whose land becomes appropriate for large-scale development. 'We have aimed to use their journey as a means to show the difficulties that landowners face in delivering high-quality housing,' said Knight Frank. 'From the complications of land equalisation, the inability to fund a planning application and the length of the planning process, to the burden that the financing of infrastructure places on large-scale development.'

The landowners are a third-generation, arable farmer and his wife. They are in their mid-thirties and have two young children. The family farm is on the edge of Fineborough, a town in middle England. The farm extends to approximately 300 acres. Fineborough is approximately 100 miles from London and fifty miles from Birmingham. The town has a population of 25,000 people, which has increased by 15% since the turn of the millennium. Over eighty-four pages, Knight Frank details the trials and tribulations faced by the family over a decade trying to develop 100 of their 300 acres. The family and town are, of course, fictional. A good way to tell a tale.

THREE

FAULTS and FACTOIDS

'Democracy is the art and science of running the circus from the monkey cage.'

H. L. Mencken

There is a housing crisis. Houses cost too much. More homes are needed. Volume housebuilders build most homes. They complain about planning red tape and land shortages. So, the red tape must be cut and more land zoned for housing. Housebuilders will then build more homes. Houses won't then cost too much. The housing crisis will end. No, it won't. These are fallacies. The conclusions do not follow from the statements. Suggesting the state can exercise control over private home building is no more than a convenient political untruth. It's deliberate absent-mindedness, knowing full well the health of the economy governs output and the private sector will always favour shareholders over society.

From this convenient untruth flows four fallacies: one – not enough homes are being built; two – more new homes will bring down the price of all homes; three: – tinkering with planning pipework will see more homes flow; four – prefabrication is the answer.

The state does exercise control over homes built by housing associations and councils. The state can encourage the supply of affordable homes by demanding a percentage of those built privately are 'affordable'. The state pays for infrastructure to make land viable for those looking to profit. Control over zoning gives the state the ability to grant or deny permission and capture part of the increase in land value to benefit society. But that's about the limit of state power.

Whitehall faults

In February 2017, Theresa May produced her administration's housing policy wrapped up in a 'white paper' called 'Fixing Our Broken Housing Market'. The former Home Secretary had been Prime Minister for seven months, elected unopposed as leader of the ruling Conservative Party in July 2016 after the resignation of David Cameron, who had fallen on his sword after finding himself on the losing side in the Brexit referendum. May's foreword signalled a break with homeowning-first philosophy of the Cameron government, which had bet the house on 'Starter Homes' and Help to Buy.

'Our broken housing market is one of the greatest barriers to progress in Britain today,' said May, 'whether buying or renting, the fact is that housing is increasingly unaffordable – particularly for ordinary working-class people who are struggling to get by.' The 106-page set of policies was pulled together by the Department for Communities and Local Government (CLG), the ministry responsible for housing. The Secretary of State at CLG, Sajid Javid, said in his introduction, 'This country doesn't have enough homes. That's not a personal opinion or a political calculation. It's a simple statement of fact.'

He then got stuck in, sounding for all the world like a Labour housing minister. 'For decades, the pace of housebuilding has been sluggish at best. As a result, the number of new homes has not kept pace with our growing population. And that, in turn, has created a market that fails to work for far too many people. Soaring prices and rising rents caused by a shortage of the right homes in the right places has slammed the door of the housing market in the face of a whole generation.' Javid lost his job as Chancellor in early 2020 for refusing to have the Treasury kowtow to Downing Street.

Back in 2017, he exhibited similar independence of mind. 'Over the years, the response from politicians has been piecemeal. Well-intentioned initiatives have built more homes here and there but have skirted around the edges of a growing problem. Other schemes have helped to tackle the symptoms without addressing the root cause. That has to change. We need radical, lasting reform that will get more homes built right now and for many years to come. The housing market has taken decades to reach the state it's now in. Turning it around won't be quick or easy. But it can be done. It must be done.'

Javid presses harder

At the Conservative Party Conference in Manchester in the first week of October 2017, Theresa May coughed through her speech but did promise to 'dedicate her premiership to fixing the broken housing market', using the spring white paper as a blueprint. Encouraged by the Prime Minister's tone, Sajid Javid sent Mrs May what became known in Whitehall lore as 'the muscular letter' on 10th October.

'We have to deliver between 225,000 and 275,000 homes every year. There's no one single magic bullet that can fix the problem. And we have to start right now... We are going to introduce a new way of assessing housing need. Many councils work tirelessly to engage their communities on the number, design and mix of new housing in their area.

'But some duck the difficult decisions and fail to produce plans that meet their housing need. The second area of focus is all about speeding up the rate of build-out. At the moment we're simply not building quickly enough. Whether it's caused by unacceptable land-banking or slow construction, we will no longer tolerate such unjustified delays. We will speed up and simplify the completion notice process.

'We will make the planning system more open and accessible. We will improve the coordination of public investment

in infrastructure and support timely connections to utilities. And we will tackle unnecessary delays caused by everything from planning conditions to great crested newts. We'll be giving developers a lot of help to get building. At present, around 60% of new homes are built by just ten companies. Small independent builders can find it almost impossible to enter the market. This lack of competition means a lack of innovation, which in turn leads to sluggish productivity growth. We will make it easier for small and medium-sized builders to compete. We will support efficient, innovative and under-used methods of construction, such as off-site factory builds. We will also support housing associations to build more, and explore options to encourage local authorities to build again, including through accelerated construction schemes on public sector land.'

Chancellor, Sajid Javid

Gavin Barwell

Working largely out of the public eye on the white paper was Gavin Barwell. The career politician became MP for the marginal seat of Croydon Central in 2010. When Theresa May became Prime Minister in the summer of 2016, Barwell was appointed Housing Minister under Javid, a post he held until losing his marginal seat in June 2017. The Prime Minister had called a snap election in a failed attempt to boost her majority. May then appointed Barwell Chief of Staff at No 10, a post he held for just over two years. Ousted along with his boss in July 2019, he was replaced by Dominic Cummings. Barwell was given a peerage and now sits in the House of Lords as Lord Barwell. His perspective is illuminating.

'The most important starting point of the white paper was the title,' says Lord Barwell. 'To get the government to say clearly, unequivocally, that we've got a broken housing market – and we are facing a crisis. Governments are always reluctant to own up to these things. My first day as Minister I had to answer questions in the House of Commons.

The line I was given was to try and pretend that the situation wasn't as bad as it actually was. But, I don't think you're ever going to have any credibility unless you start from a position of being honest.'

How the machine works

Lord Barwell explains how the Whitehall machine worked. 'There were three key actors in the production of the white paper. The first was the Department for Communities and Local Government. Sajid was very passionate about getting housing numbers up to 300,000, if not beyond. The second was No 10, which I think shared the view there was a broken market. But advisors were nervous about some of the more radical ideas, like building on the green belt. Then there was the Treasury, who also thought there was a problem but felt the problem was with the planning system – and that there wasn't anything wrong with the market. And they certainly didn't need to put up any more money. This was the triangle: HM Treasury, who wanted planning reform; No 10 were interested in market reform; and Sajid and I were sort of saying, "Well, we actually need both." How that argument played out between those three parts is probably the key to understanding the context in which the white paper was published.'

Gavin Barwell admits that ideas he and Sajid Javid wanted in the white paper were lost to expediency. 'We wanted a firm commitment to look at land value capture. A review would then have given a pretty clear inclination of the direction of travel. The Treasury was not keen on this, and it got pushed into the long grass, essentially. Another thing on which No 10 and CLG would have gone further – absent the Treasury – was on council housing and the funding for affordable housing. The Treasury has a perfectly rational view. It's cheaper for the government to have housing associations build than having councils do the work, as housing associations are not on the public balance sheet. Our point was, "That's all very well, but the truth is there is a limit to the capacity of the housing association sector to build homes. We need to get councils building as well, then we're going to get extra homes. There is a limit to either the ambition or the capacity of associations to build new homes."'

Lord Barwell says, in retrospect, 'the biggest weakness of the white paper is that it didn't have an answer at all for parts of the north of England. There are parts of the country where there isn't a supply crisis. Where rents in the private sector are very similar to rents in the social renting sector. And the crisis there is often poor-quality stock that needs renovation. If you've got a local authority estate that needs completely refurbishing you can't pay for it by increasing density by putting more housing in, because there isn't the demand for the additional units. What's the answer there? But the overall balance of the white paper still stands the test of time. I still think the multi-tenure answer is the right answer.'

Dysfunctional decision-making

'How the government seeks to reach a collective agreement on these things can be completely dysfunctional,' admits Lord Barwell. 'What happens is you, within the department, draw up your first draft of what this white paper is going to look like. Then you run it around to the other affected departments, saying, "This is what we propose to do. What do you think?" And people write back with comments. It drove me nuts. Sajid was in charge. But his relationship with No 10 was quite difficult. So, I was doing a lot of brokering behind the scenes with No 10. Then there were the officials in the Treasury, who were advising [the Chancellor] Philip [Hammond].

'But you couldn't ever get to meet them. I was like, "Why can't we just get a meeting? Well, why don't we invite over Nick Timothy [Mrs May's joint Chief of Staff] from No 10. Invite Treasury officials, and we all sit around the table and we sort this out?"

'There was one particular issue one weekend when we were getting close to finalising the text. A letter came through from the Treasury, saying, "Change this bit in this way." Another letter came through from No 10 telling us to change the same bit in the opposite direction.' And you just sort of sat there, thinking, "Well, what are we going to do now, then?" The Prime Minister can ultimately insist on money from their Chancellor, but it's partly a function of the relationship between No 10 and No 11, which was not in a good place then.'

In mid-August 2020 the government published 'Planning for the Future,' billed as the most radical set of changes to the planning system since the 1947 Act. Housing Secretary, Robert Jenrick repeated the factoid - that better planning equals more homes. 'These proposals will help build the homes our country needs, bridge the generational divide and recreate an ownership society in which more people have the dignity and security of a home of their own.'

The proposed changes themselves are clever, at least at first blush. The government dictates the number of homes each council has to build. No more prevarication at local level. This should help cut the time land becomes available for homes. The government dictates the level of a new "infrastructure levy' to replace both Section 106 payments and the Community Land Tax. A chance to disarm and demob the army of experts making a living from sterile arguments over how many angels can perch on a brick. Better still, the tax is only payable 'on occupation.' Developers don't have to pay until they get the money. But, critically, 'occupation' by sale or rent establishes the value on which the tax is levied. No more guessing games.

It gets better for developers, worse for councils who may have to wait years for their tax money. The latter have to draw up maps delineating land as either 'growth areas' or 'renewal areas' or 'protected areas.' Councils then have to post this upon a developer accessible map along with 'pattern books' of what sort of homes they like. Fit the pattern in the Growth Area and, bingo, automatic outline planning. No, it's not going to be that easy. Especially as the government has yoked the plans to a very smelly donkey: the expansion of Permitted Development Rights. A policy that allows developers convert what the Guardian calls 'the slums of tomorrow.'

It's the economy, stupid

The supply and demand for private homes is controlled by economic forces, not political actions. Look at the data from the last three major recessions. UK private housing starts fell by a third between 1976 and 1981, down from 153,000 to 102,000. Between 1986 and 1991, they fell 20% to 139,000. Between 2006 and 2009, the number plunged by more than half, from 205,000 to 89,000. The last thing on the mind of volume builders at these times was hoarding land. The only crisis housebuilders had was their own. How to survive. The coronavirus crisis of 2020 is the latest test.

A smarter way to guess

An economist from Mars might suggest estimates of private output should be based on an algorithm, predicting what the private sector could supply, rather than what politicians would like them to supply. A formula linking historic output, economic confidence, GDP and past levels of output, perhaps? Deduct that number from the number your chosen political party thinks the country needs, and you have what the state must supply.

Understanding what the private sector is prepared to supply is discussed under 'Factoids' later in this Chapter, then, more fully, in Chapter Seven. What planning reformers fail to understand is that the price of new homes is determined by two interacting markets. Think of an old-style gasometer. The 'lid' cannot rise above the level determined by the giant hand in the sky, which eases and squeezes prices as the economy rises and falls. The gasometer has two chambers. The top relatively inflexible chamber contains fixed costs and profit margins. The lower flexible chamber is the price of land. If the hand squeezes the lid, land prices fall. If the hand eases the lid, land prices rise. The price of new homes, however many are supplied, is determined by the giant hand of the economy, not by the supply of more land.

Labour policy

In April 2018, Labour borrowed from the Conservative phrasebook in their policy document 'Housing for the Many', using the same phrase we borrowed to give the title to this book. 'The housing market is broken,' said Shadow Housing Secretary John Healey, in the foreword. 'After eight long years, it is clear that the current Conservative housing policy is failing to fix it.' The party is unlikely to be back in power until the mid-2020s. Does Healey think the policy laid down in April 2018 will change much now Labour has a new leader in Keir Starmer?

'No,' said Healey, while still Shadow Housing Secretary. 'We went back to first principles. We made the arguments. We've been building allies for those arguments. Whether it's backbench Tory MPs or Conservative council leaders. Compared to four years ago, they're now making many of the same arguments as us. In a sense, we're winning those arguments. I fundamentally believe we have answers to the country's housing crisis and the government does not. And these arguments and these answers are now increasingly seen as common sense. They may be radical in places, but they're also credible and deliverable. And that's the task of opposition – to continue to press that case.' Starmer subsequently promoted Healey to the defence brief. His April 2020 replacement is Bristol West MP Thangam Debbonaire, whose First in Mathematics from Oxford should prove useful.

Faulty thought processes

Lord Barwell admitted earlier that policy development can be 'totally dysfunctional'. Former Labour Housing Minister Nick Raynsford (1997–2001) points his finger at the fact that there have been nineteen housing ministers since 1997. 'There is an obvious problem when ministers are only in post for very short periods – and we've had that problem in spades in the last twenty years. You have no chance whatsoever of getting a coherent and sensible policy approach because ministers will have no time to get their heads around the subject and understand the long-term implications of proposed changes.

'Instead, they will be only interested in short-term measures, shiny little initiatives that can carry their name and be seen as their legacy. You don't get housing results by shiny short-term initiatives. You've got to have policies that can really deliver over time. I was responsible, among other things, for the Decent Homes programme, which had a very significant impact on the condition of millions of existing social homes, which had been allowed to deteriorate through inadequate maintenance over a long period. It took a ten-year time span to make the impact it did. That's the timescale that is often necessary for delivering housing.

'Policy-making today tends to be a long way away from a sensible and rational process. What tends to happen is you get a bright idea dreamed up, usually by a think tank. The think tank talks to key politicians, who evaluate whether or not it's going to have political appeal. And if they like it, they will then get it worked up by people who probably have no technical expertise in the subject whatsoever, and no ability to reach an informed judgement as to whether or not it might succeed in the real world, as well as what unforeseen consequences might flow from its adoption. On this flimsy basis, it is put in a party's manifesto because it is thought to be likely to be attractive to a section of the electorate. It is then treated as if it were Holy Writ which must be implemented because it's a manifesto commitment.

'Virtually none of this is how you should make good policy, which is to get people who are experts to consider the issues, to analyse the options, to refine them, test them, see where there are problems and unforeseen consequences, work out whether these can be overcome, and anticipate how the new policy is likely to impact those people or organisations at whom it is directed. Then, after a period of intense consultation with the organisations which will have to implement the policy, provisional plans can be drawn up, including the pilot, before the policy is implemented – with the scope to make changes if the policy doesn't work out as expected. Most businesses work this way.'

'It's a bit like being cast as Doctor Who,' says Mark Prisk, who was Housing Minister between September 2012 and October 2013. 'You're quietly getting on with ministerial business. Then this very excited, very enthusiastic group of young people come rushing in, wanting to do lots of different things. You're thinking, Right, OK, I don't want to be wholly negative. You allow them to run with some of their thoughts. An enormous amount of energy then goes into developing their suggestions.

Then, suddenly they are off, onto the next subject. And as a minister of state, you're usually left trying to pick up the pieces.

'It's partly the appetite of the twenty-four-hour press and politicians want to be seen doing something new. It's not good enough to be doing what the previous minister was doing or doing it better or quicker. There's always a demand for "something must be done" policies,' says Prisk. Here is one of the worst examples.

Faulty starter homes

The Chancellor's Autumn Statement was late coming in 2014. Not till December did George Osborne set out the next Big Housing Idea: Starter Homes. In April 2015, the Conservative manifesto committed to '200,000 Starter Homes, which will be sold at a 20% discount and will be built exclusively for first-time buyers under 40'.

'I think I'm sort of partially responsible for something that I disapproved of,' admits Lord Barwell, referring to the programme. 'Both David [Cameron] and George [Osborne] came down and campaigned for me in the 2015 election. Both asked me, "Why do you think we're struggling in London?"

'My answer was that, "it's partly demography. And it's partly about housing." The decline in homeownership had been a lot steeper in London than elsewhere. I think they took from the conversation a zeal for trying to reverse the decline in homeownership. Housing policy almost became solely focused on that. There wasn't really an offering to people in the private rental sector or people who were going to need council housing or special housing.'

The November 2015 Spending Review subsequently provided £2.3 billion to support the delivery of 60,000 of these homes. I was writing for *Planning* magazine at the time. In an attempt to show how housebuilders might react, I invented a conversation between the directors of a volume housebuilder, watching the Chancellor on TV, as he rose to his feet in the House of Commons:

'We are the builders now,' declared the Chancellor in the Commons to cheers.

'No, you are bloody not,' shouted the MD of MegaMini Homes at the eighty-five inch Samsung hung on the boardroom wall. 'We are!' Sitting around the table alongside the MD were the directors of finance, sales and planning, all nodding.

MD: 'I spoke to the bugger last week. I know, I know, we're only one year into a five-year plan to grow sales at 10% compound, from 10,000 a year to 16,000 by 2020. George says we have to take the lead, show an example. George suggests we should up our output to 20,000 units a year by 2020, with half being starter and shared ownership homes.'

FD: '"George"? Very cosy. What are you after, a bloody knighthood? We will have to add half a billion to our borrowing to fund the extra construction, costs of which are already skyrocketing. Imagine the fun the brick-makers are going to have. As for getting labour... well, we'll have to double our recruitment budget in the Baltics.'

Sales director: 'Calm down. I have a plan. We can re-designate the poorer/smaller parts of upcoming phases as "starter" homes. Our guys are already working on a plan that will push up the prices on private sales and squeeze down the size and so pack in more of these starter units. A combination that will enable us to show the required 20% discount.'

MD: 'I have reached a decision. We nearly went bankrupt in 2008, when the market crashed. Bugger the knighthood. Let's stick with the original plan. But market the smaller units as starter homes and grab the money for doing so. If the market crashes? We stop work. Ours is not to do the politicians bidding.'

Planning, December 2014

Promises, promises

In May 2015 the Conservatives won an outright majority, then promised to build one million homes by 2020, including 200,000 of the new starter homes. I was asked by the home-selling website OnTheMarket to explain to potential buyers what was going on:

> *'Well, here we are, the Conservative Party is in power for five years. Their manifesto promises to hit two big housing targets by 2020. First, the erection of 200,000 "quality starter homes", units reserved for first-time buyers under forty, sold at 20% below open market prices. Second, 275,000 "affordable" units. Councils will be ordered to identify all brownfield sites in their locale. They will be told to grant builders planning permission on 90% of these sites by 2020. In the capital, a London Land Commission has already been set up. Housing zones will be identified and land enough to build 95,000 new homes will be found.*
>
> *'How councils persuade those who build houses to comply with this detailed interventionist agenda is not discussed. The only thing missing from the strategy are the words "Five-Year Plan". Stalin had slave labour to ensure his wishes were executed. Politicians have no more control over the new homes market than they have over the mushroom market. Yet the myth persists that all that needs to be done is to create the right soil conditions and builders will come.'*

OnTheMarket, May 2015

Starter homes were still official policy when plain Gavin Barwell took over as Housing Minister in the summer of 2016. He began to edge away from the policy. 'It was not easy to just walk away from something that was in the manifesto. But we had several concerns. You'd have been providing one form of housing at the expense of other forms of housing. The second concern was, you were giving a big discount to some lucky people who pocketed their discount. So, when they sold the home, it wasn't an affordable home for local people anymore. We were pretty clear, privately, that the number of starter homes that were going to be built would be much, much lower. That didn't bother us. What did bother us was, what's the total pool of housing, either homeownership or affordable rent we're going to get?'

National audit office investigation

In November 2019, the National Audit Office exposed the whole plan as a shambles. The conclusions were devastating: not a single starter home had been started, five years after George Osborne's Big Idea was born. Funding originally intended for starter homes was instead spent on acquiring public land. Between 2015 and 2018, £172m was spent. In January 2020, the Johnson administration signalled the scheme was to be officially buried.

'It was such a disaster because it came in from nowhere,' says Mark Prisk, who gave up his seat of Hertford and Stortford in November 2019 after nineteen years as a Conservative MP. 'The policy was dragged into the Communities and Local Government department against many of our wishes. No 10 had somehow persuaded the Treasury this was a good idea. It sounded great. Ticked all the boxes. Who doesn't want starter homes for young people? Why would you not want that? It's mom and apple pie. But the problem was it was completely ill-considered. These sorts of things come out of the blue. You, as the minister, get to take it through to Parliament. Starter homes were foisted on Brandon Lewis, who had to deal with it.'

Labour record

There is a steadfast belief among all parties that clearing 'the planning system' will unblock a geyser of new homes. This was the central assumption of Labour's housing policy between 1997 and 2011. One Labour minister was not convinced – and lost his job. 'I resisted the proposed change to the system', says Nick Raynsford, 'because my view was the existing system was not bust. It did need some improvement around the edges, but it was capable of being reformed. And I thought that the risk of throwing all the balls up in the air was far too great. So, I resisted it, which is one of the reasons Charlie Falconer became Minister for Housing and Planning in 2001. I was moved off to something else. I was seen to be unhelpful.' Raynsford moved to work for John Prescott at the Office of the Deputy Prime Minister and became Minister for London.

Falconer for breakfast

That same year, Falconer came to one of the regular breakfasts *Estates Gazette* hosted in the basement of John Gummer's house, adjacent to the Home Office. Gummer wrote a weekly column for *Estates Gazette* for nearly a decade, until 2009. The new Planning Minister had come to tell of plans for the 'biggest planning revolution since 1947'. Gummer was then MP for Suffolk Coastal, a man best known to the public for feeding his daughter a beef burger in 1990 when Secretary of State for Agriculture, in an attempt to calm fears about mad cow disease. He swapped to Environment Secretary in 1993 and held the post until 1997 when Tony Blair arrived. Inside Westminster, he was known as an early apostle of climate change policy. As Lord Deben, Gummer was appointed chairman of the UK's independent Committee on Climate Change, a post he still held in 2020.

These two formidable opponents sparred over bacon and eggs in front of a small audience. Gummer quizzed Falconer hard. But the Labour QC had mastered his brief. Falconer made a compelling case for wholesale reform of the planning system. His assumption that fixing the planning system would cure housing ills underpinned the Planning Act of 2004 – and the series of reports by economist Kate Barker. Almost every one of the thirty-two recommendations in her final report in December 2006 focused on fixing planning as if fixing the plumbing would increase water supply.

Factoids

Factoids were defined by the American author of The Naked and the Dead, Norman Mailer, in his 1973 biography of Marilyn Monroe. Mailer described a factoid as an 'item of unreliable information that is reported and repeated so often that it becomes accepted as fact'.

Factoid one: Britain has a housing crisis

Emotive topic. Here are the facts. There were 24.4 million dwellings in England on 31st March 2019, an increase of 241,000 dwellings on the same point the previous year. The number of new homes needed to absorb changes in population and changing living habits is 170,000, says the Office for National Statistics, suggesting that will bring quite enough extra homes each year between 2020 and 2040. But of no comfort to those who cannot afford to buy or rent at market prices. There were 88,000 families in temporary accommodation as of December 2019 and 1.15 million folks on council house waiting lists. Neither group is likely to ever have the money to either buy or rent a home at anything much above half the market rent. For this group, there is a terrible, undeniable crisis.

If you are between the age of twenty-five and forty and unable to get onto the first rung of the housing ladder, there is also a housing crisis. If prices are eighteen times the average salary, there is a housing crisis. Prices are too high. But is the crisis the fault of housebuilders charging too much? They charge what the market bears, just like pencil-makers. The amount they charge is linked to the price of second-hand homes. Those living in second-hand homes can hardly be expected to sell at below market prices. Why should housebuilders? There is an affordability crisis, not a supply crisis.

Factoid two: building more homes will lower prices

To repeat, there were 24.4 million homes in England in 2019, 241,000 more than the year before. Might increasing the flow to 300,000 bring down prices? Unlikely – new homes are like new cars. Buyers pay more. The price of a new home tends to lie between 15% and 20% above that of used stock.

Take the argument down to the local level. Pick a town containing 50,000 homes, with an average value of £250,000 each. Anytown adds 500 new homes in one year, adding 1% to its stock. They sell for an average of £300,000 each. On which planet would this activity lower the general price of homes? The reality is prices step up and down to the level of demand, which dances to the tune of the economy.

Factoid three: improving planning will bring forth more homes

Improvements to the planning system have never, ever contributed to more homes being built. The 'planning system' is like the tax system – it can always be improved. Improvements to increase the supply of land are fine and dandy. But what then gets built is an entirely separate matter. The land banks of the top six housebuilders rose by 10,000 between 2017 and 2018 to over 350,000 despite selling over 70,000 homes at carefully controlled rates of under one per week. As the table shows, each likes to hold four or six years of land to help plan, not to hoard.

Land banks, land supply, outlets, sales per outlet per week (SPOW)

	2017/18	2018/19	2017/18	2018/19	2017/18	2018/19	2018/19
	Plots		Land supply, years		Outlets		SPOW
Barratt	79,432	80,022	4.8	4.7	380	379	0.7
Persimmon	98,445	99,098	6.1	6	375	360	0.75
Taylor Wimpey	74,849	76,000	5.4	5.1	288	256	0.8
Bellway	41,077	42,721	2.4	2.4	247	268	1.2
Redrow	27,630	31,500	4.8	4.9	124	129	0.96
Countryside	19,778	24,304	4.6	4.2	53	56	0.84
Totals	341,211	353,645			1,467	1,448	

Source: company accounts

Factoid four: pre-fab homes can solve the UK's housing crisis

Prefabrication can be a good thing. The process of building components in factories has been redubbed Modern Methods of Construction. MMC is a good way of ensuring factory-standard kitchens and bathrooms. But the idea that prefabrication will 'solve Britain's housing crisis' is nonsense. Yet in early 2020, Junior Housing Minister Esther McVey was suggesting that the 'industrialisation of housebuilding offers a unique opportunity to drive affordability into the sector which can then, in turn, be passed on to the house buyer'. The misconception promoted by MMC suppliers is that because you can build faster and more cheaply, more homes will be built and sold at lower prices.

Cost and efficiency savings accrue to the seller. Why on earth would they sell or rent below market price? The idea that the consumer will benefit is moonshine. The idea that because you can build more quickly means you will sell more quickly is also a complete disconnect, as housebuilders' steady sales rates per site per week (SPOW) rates show. A more serious misconception put about by the promoters of prefabrication is that the public housing tenants will benefit, making affordable homes even more affordable. There may be a case that cost savings mean a social provider can build ten homes for the price of nine and they will go up a bit faster. Granted, a benefit to the provider of homes and, OK, yes to families on the waiting list. But that still does not mean the rent the tenant pays will be less, because the house is bolted together.

FOUR

THE GHOSTS IN THE MACHINE

'Houses are built to live in, and not to look on: therefore, let use be preferred before uniformity.'

Francis Bacon

The ghosts in the housing machine are the occupants. Those who buy or rent new homes are real enough, but living in ways scarcely seen, understood or researched. Hunt the housing literature, white papers, National Planning Policy Frameworks, the pronouncements of professional bodies, think tank essays or the agendas of good-intentioned housing conferences. The occupants are spectral figures, barely regarded, rarely discussed, or, if mentioned, patronised. They are seen only as customers by the private sector and suppliants by the public sector – either way, expected to fit rather than form the mould.

A century ago the wellbeing of occupants moulded thinking. Towards the end of the First World War, architect and MP Sir John Tudor Walters was asked by the government to create blueprints for homes fit for working-class people.

'You cannot expect to get an A1 population out of C3 homes,' he said, referring to military fitness classifications. His report was published in 1918, recommending the setting of mandatory standards for public housing. These findings were incorporated into the 1919 Addison Act, named after Dr Christopher Addison, Minister for Reconstruction until January 1919, when he became President of the local government board. In March 1919, he put in an order for 300 million bricks and told the demobilisation department to get men out of uniform and into the brickyards. He abolished his role five months later to become the first Minister for Health, the department responsible for the first Housing and Town Planning Act.

Medical opinion

The attention paid by the Ministry of Health to the occupants permeates the policy. 'Medical opinion is unanimous as to the importance of sunshine to penetrate the rooms.' Tudor Walters produced five model plans. Not that many were ever built. But his layouts informed council house plans until the 1950s. Maximum densities were laid down. No more than twelve to the acre (thirty to the hectare) in urban areas and eight to the acre (twenty to the hectare) in rural areas. Metrics were set that kept density levels down. 'Housing is to be in short terraces, spaced seventy feet apart, to allow the penetration of sunlight even in winter,' said Tudor Walters. 'These terraces should be a maximum of eight houses long. Deep narrow-fronted terraces to be avoided as they reduce airflow and light to the back of the house.' For all but the smallest two models, he recommended a frontage of twenty-two feet six inches, six to ten feet wider than many of today's new homes.

Minimum internal sizes were laid down. Model A was 755 square feet, sixteen feet wide on plan. This space did not include a kitchen, nor a bathroom nor dining room. Just a scullery. A range for cooking was installed in a living (and eating) room. The privy stood outside. The same layout for the seventeen-foot wide Model B gave 855 square feet of space. The recommended size for a three-bed four-person home today? One that includes a kitchen and bathroom and inside toilet – 904 square feet.

Model C in the Tudor Walters range was 1,055 square feet, standing twenty-four feet wide by twenty-one feet deep. A parlour had been added. 'A quiet room for reading, writing to a sick relative or formal entertaining of non-family visitors.' The D and E models were the same size, different layout. Imagine how little *stuff* a poor family had in 1919. Yet three of the five model semi-detached homes were as big as many detached homes are today. We've also grown. The average male in 1919 was five feet seven inches and weighed eleven stone. Today the average man is two inches taller and two stone heavier.

Today's standards

Nationally Described Space Standards (NDSS) were introduced in October 2015. At the end of her premiership, in June 2019, Theresa May called for these standards to be made mandatory. Her housing advisor Toby Lloyd helped pull together the speech 'and did a fair bit of badgering inside government', he admits, before May spoke to a Chartered Institute of Housing conference in Manchester.

'I want to see changes to regulations so that developers can only build homes that are big enough for people to live in. It was the Addison Act that brought modern space standards to English housing law for the first time. During the bill's second reading, the architect of the standards, Sir Tudor Walters, urged MPs to "take care that the houses planned in the future are planned with due regard to comfort, convenience and the saving of labour". It is a message we would do well to return to today. Because in the years since, the pendulum has swung back and forth between regulation and deregulation, leading to a situation today where England does have national standards – but largely unenforceable ones.

'Some local authorities include the Nationally Described Space Standard in their local plans. But, others do not. And even where they are applied, they are open to negotiation. I cannot defend a system in which some owners and tenants are forced to accept tiny homes with inadequate storage. Where developers feel the need to fill show homes with deceptively small furniture. And where the lack of universal standards encourage a race to the bottom. It will be up to my successor in Downing Street to deal with this.'

Nationally Described Space Standards (NDSS)

Square feet					Square metres
		Storey			(for max sizes)
Bedrooms	Occupants	One	Two	Three	
1	1	398			37
1	2	538	624		58
2	3	657	753		70
2	4	753	850		79
3	4	797	904	969	90
3	5	926	1,001	1,066	99
3	6	1,023	1,098	1,163	108
4	5	969	1,044	1,109	103
4	6	1,066	1,141	1,206	112
4	7	1,163	1,238	1,302	121
4	8	1,259	1,335	1,399	130
5	6	1,109	1,184	1,249	116
5	7	1,206	1,281	1,346	125
5	8	1,302	1,378	1,442	134
6	7	1,249	1,324	1,389	129
6	8	1,346	1,421	1,485	138

Source: MHCLG

What was just about the Prime Minister's last public speech ended: 'I believe the next government should be bold enough to ensure the Nationally Described Space Standard applies to all new homes. And bring an end to the era of too-small homes that are barely fit for modern family life. I reject the argument that such a change will make building less likely.' May was echoing the thoughts of Toby Lloyd who had overseen a report called 'New Civic Housebuilding' while working at Shelter.

Shelter goes to the heart of the matter

Shelter had addressed the size issue back in 2013 when Lloyd was head of policy. 'Little Boxes, Fewer Homes' maintained that if developers built bigger and better homes they would meet less resistance at the planning stage. Research by the charity showed 73% of people would support housing developments if homes were better designed and in keeping with the local area. 'Even those that did not see the need for more homes are more likely to support a development with larger homes, with minimum space standards, compared to one with smaller homes.' Shelter then speared the heart of the matter. 'If the regulations required mandatory space standards, the additional development cost would become a non-negotiable factor in land purchases, making it possible for developers to build the sort of homes that people want to see without threatening the viability of the development or reducing the affordability of the homes.'

Former Housing Minister Mark Prisk, who read Land Economy at Reading before joining Knight Frank as a graduate trainee, worries that competition for land is squeezing down sizes. 'We are building some homes that are frankly too small. I visited some sites where the proverbial cat wouldn't survive even in the living room. I think there is an argument for saying that we ought to have some simpler rules – but robust ones – and space standards are a good example.'

Sir Parker Morris

Planners tend to play God with ghostly occupants. Sir Parker Morris did, back in 1961, when the senior civil servant drew up the most widely recalled set of standards. His grid has been used ever since as a template, including by the Greater London Authority. In 2006 in a review of its standards, the GLA admitted, 'There is no way of knowing what the level of occupancy will be over the life of the property.' Guessing the number of bed spaces is done with good intent, says expert Julia Park, an architect at Levitt Bernstein who authored 'One Hundred Years of Housing Space Standards' in 2017. The GLA standard was devised to stem the tide of small flats. Before the crash of 2007/08, one-bedroom flats of forty to forty-five square metres were commonplace. Two-bedroom flats were typically sixty-two to sixty-seven square metres. More enlightened planners realised that for anything to change, the one-bedroom flats had to meet the two-person standard of fifty square metres, and a proportion of two-bedroom flats had to meet the four-person standard of seventy square metres.'

Parker Morris: minimum metres square (storage of 2.8 to 4.6 metres square not included)

| Type | Persons | | | | | |
	One	Two	Three	Four	Five	Six
Three-storey houses					98.3	97.5
Two-story terraces				74.3	84.5	92.0
Two-storey semis				71.5	81.8	92.0
Flat	29.7	44.6	56.7	69.7	79.0	86.4
Single-storey house	29.7	44.6	56.7	66.8	75.2	83.6

Source: 1961 Parker Morris standards for public housing

Ikea land

Furniture size guidelines which inform the NDSS standards seem divorced from the way we live now. Settees – 1,850 millimetres by 800 millimetres deep. A dining table for four – 800 millimetres by 1,200 millimetres. A double bed – no wider than 1,500 millimetres. The width of wardrobe space for one person – 600 millimetres. Who can stuff their clothes into that amount of space? A working-class Victorian, with one Sunday suit? This size of furniture can be found in an IKEA showroom. But go to Rightmove or any other website where photographs of homes for sale are displayed. Take a look at how people actually furnish small houses. Squishy couches up to three metres long sit opposite huge TV screens. As in Victorian times, families eat in the living room, usually on the settee. Peek in the bedrooms. Multiple chests of drawers belie the belief that the storage space is adequate.

Boris to the rescue

An unlikely champion of space standards strode on to the stage in the summer of 2008. Not only did this hero want to adopt Parker Morris standards, but he also wanted to enlarge them by 10%. I dubbed them Parker-Boris standards. At the time, my stage was a weekly page in the City section of the *Evening Standard*. I went to see the Mayor of London make a speech and wrote this:

'One mild evening last week, Boris Johnson joined 1,000 or so members of the design community, who were milling around in the quadrangle of Somerset House munching pizza and gossiping. The Mayor blurted out a speech, squinting occasionally at notes clenched in his fist, then quickly left. Boris does tend to rush from one witticism to the next when speaking. But there are occasional half-apologetic pauses when he glances at the prepared text and says something unfunny – but interesting.

'"I want to re-establish the space standards set by Sir Parker Morris in 1961," was the interesting remark. Interesting because it could force housebuilders to increase the size of new homes in London; interesting because it could force down the price of building land. The not-so-casual pledge has its roots in a report called Housing Space Standards, commissioned by Ken Livingstone and published in August 2006. The main recommendation was indeed to build to Parker Morris standards. Nearly half a century later, builders are putting up one-bed flats as small as 300 square feet, two-bed units of 445 square feet and three-bed ones at 657 square feet. These are the very smallest examples uncovered by London Residential Research, which says the average one-bed flat has shrunk by 13% since 2000.

'Each square foot a builder saves shaves at least £150 off building costs. A 300 square foot, one-bedroom flat costs about £45,000 to build. The minimum 490 square foot flat built to Parker Morris standards will cost £73,500 – 63% more. This extra £28,500 will either shrink profits – or shrink the price of the land, if not already bought and paid for. English Partnerships was so concerned by the shrinking British flat last year that it now demands all units it subsidises are built 10% bigger than the Parker Morris minimum.

'Ken was less concerned. Last September, his draft housing policy was published. There was a passing reference to Sir Parker's ideas "being tailored to meet the requirements of living in today's London", but then a dismissive "there is already a plethora of standards – and the Mayor has no wish to add to their number". Will this mayor?'

27th June 2008, *Evening Standard*

Boris for Prime Minister

In May 2009, Boris Johnson was true to his word. I was so excited by the news that I suggested he should be made Prime Minister, at the very least (a wild idea at the time):

'Hooray for Boris. Make the Mayor of London Prime Minister, no, King. For our hero seems to have faced down penny-pinching housebuilders to insist no more rabbit-hutch homes be built for sale in London. This news is tucked away on page forty-four of an otherwise dull eighty-eight-page review of London's planning laws. After some preliminary waffle about requiring the "highest-quality design standards", Boris Johnson is fairly specific: "these new requirements will include minimum space standards."

'The minimum space standards the Mayor is talking about will outlaw the 300 square foot studio flat and ban builders from squeezing two bedrooms into flats sometimes as small as 500 square feet. Instead, the minimum size for a one-bed flat will be 550 square feet. Those with two bedrooms must be no smaller than

770 square feet. Housebuilders who have run a campaign against the idea will be furious. For it will cost them around £150 for every extra square foot to comply with the "Parker Morris plus 10%" rule.

'There is some wriggle room in what should surely be dubbed the Parker-Boris standard in honour of our hero. But, if the development contains private and housing association flats, the private flats will have to be at least as big as the flats subsidised with government money. The Parker-Boris standard has already been adopted by the biggest builder of new homes in London today: the government's very own Homes and Communities Agency. It's an agency with leverage, for the HCA is pouring tens of millions in public money into dozens of developments.

'One such development stands at 150 High Street, Stratford, close to the entrance to the Olympic Games. Here Genesis Housing Association had begun work on 655 new homes. A third of the 655 units are destined for Genesis clients. But more than 400 were supposed to be for private buyers. That prospect has evaporated. Genesis is in deep trouble. It has turned to the HCA for a £48 million bailout loan. Part of the price paid for the loan is the enlargement of the private flats in the tower, which has only reached the third of its forty-three storeys. Genesis was coy when asked but admits "it is true that we are reviewing this scheme and are working with the HCA to achieve the right scheme". What this means in practice is that a new firm of architects has been brought in to turn some two-bed flats into one-bed flats and enlarge the one-bed rabbit hutches that Genesis (which really, really should have known better) was going to foist on private buyers.'

8th May 2009, *Evening Standard*

There was then a rear-guard action from housebuilders, who managed to pursuade the GLA that one-person studio flats of just under 400 square feet were permissible. I was taken to one such flat in North London in April 2010 by Tony Carey, then-number two to Berkeley Group founder Tony Pidgley, who died in June 2020. Beaufort Park in Harrow stands near the tail of the M1, next door to the Metropolitan Police training HQ. The development was impressive. The studio flat was also impressive. I came away thinking, *Well, why not?* then remembered just how many mirrors there were and how oddly small the furniture looked.

Minimum standards

Should now-Prime Minister, Boris Johnson, order his Parker-Boris standards to be applied across the country? Could development appraisals stand for homes being 25% bigger and built at 20% lower density? Those questions are answered on the imaginary settlements described in Chapters One and Two. But in the real world? Johnson hinted that minimum space standards would be introduced. Lo, there is a provision in the August 2020 White Paper for local planning authorities to mould their own 'pattern books' – to define what is acceptable in their bailiwick. One of the task force members who helped frame the proposals is leading developer, Sir Stuart Lipton. He suggests that planning authorities could dictate size and density levels. 'If the council wants every home to have three parking spaces and be 22-feet wide, that's it. It's important that communities feel they are participating in planning.'

The Prime Minister would get the backing of the Resolution Foundation. In July 2020 the think tank revealed the disparities in the amount of space enjoyed by young and old. Those under 44 had around 300 square feet of liveable space per person. Those in the 55 to 64-year-old age group occupied 450 square feet per person. Numbers that only relate to the white population. Members of the Black, Asian or other ethnic minorities had significantly less space to enjoy.

Raising standards

Former Labour Housing Minister Nick Raynsford is sceptical about the idea of raising space standards. 'I am sympathetic to the case. A lot of modern housing is too small and cramped. But my argument is we don't want a one-size-fits-all approach. 'We need to be flexible to take account of different circumstances in different parts of Britain,' says Raynsford. 'There's a need to understand the aspirations of people who don't necessarily want very large units, but who want well-designed homes.'

David Birkbeck of consultancy Design for Homes denies builders cram in as many homes as they can get away with: 'Quality indicators, such as internal dimensions, are a function of local land values. Wherever developers know they'll get a return, they build bigger. Homes in Cambridge are very much bigger than those in Peterborough, homes in Horsham are bigger than those in Fareham, while places like Blackpool or Redcar have the smallest as the design is essentially the local square foot prices times four local household incomes.' Meaning, while there is no floor for standards, the poorer you are the tighter you are squeezed.

Barratt view

Philip Barnes is group land and planning director at Barratt Developments, the country's largest housebuilder. Does he feel that housebuilders have had no option but to increase densities in order to compete for land? 'It is too simplistic to assume that increasing density automatically equals a higher land value. Winning a competitive land bid requires balancing build cost and revenue. A land bid based on fifty larger plots will never win a site with capacity and consent for 100 homes.

'But equally, cramming 200 homes on the same site is similarly unlikely to win due to the huge increase in build cost, plus worsened quality of place and hence a lower revenue per square foot. Also, such site cramming is unlikely to be acceptable to the council for design reasons. A winning land bid is usually one which will both reduce risks to build cost and quality whilst also creating a community that customers will love living in.'

The great squeeze

The great squeeze on density began, slowly at first, in 1996. At the time the number of homes being built on each hectare of land in England averaged twenty-five. By the turn of the millennium it eased up to twenty-eight, then shot up to forty-one by 2004 and did not move much by 2011, when the data ends. This two-thirds rise in density levels in England is not a topic you will find widely researched. The rise in the number of flats and fall in the number of houses is the main reason. Between the wars, 56% of new homes had three beds. Today that figure is 30%. Between 1999 and 2019 the percentage of one- and two-bed flats ballooned from 15% to 49% of completions. Needless to say, it's the poorer places that saw the highest rises. The doubling, tripling and quadrupling of densities lie in the poorer parts of London.

Top 20% increase in homes per hectare, 1996–2011

Authority	1996–99	2000–03	2004–07	2008–11	1996–2011 % increase
Newham	54	80	133	271	402%
Tower Hamlets	96	138	254	385	301%
Salford	31	49	94	118	281%
Southwark	70	97	178	247	253%
Redbridge	39	39	87	125	221%
Sheffield	25	31	89	80	220%
Harrow	29	48	49	84	190%
Hackney	71	103	140	202	185%
Wandsworth	60	92	106	164	173%
Leeds	25	35	61	61	144%
Hammersmith and Fulham	70	88	139	170	143%
Sutton	34	45	47	77	126%
Liverpool	35	44	74	79	126%
Lambeth	73	89	110	157	115%
Manchester	40	66	101	86	115%
Hounslow	56	66	120	117	109%
Waltham Forest	49	39	87	100	104%
Lewisham	74	52	119	150	103%
Bristol	48	59	78	97	102%
Hillingdon	35	44	49	64	83%
England	25	28	41	42	68%

Source: ONS

Garden squeeze

The number of folks with no front or back garden has doubled since the 1980s to over 40%. That can be partially put down to the increase in the number of flats. But that excuse cannot be used to explain why gardens have also got a lot smaller. Before 1945 over 90% of gardens were longer than fifteen metres. After 2002 the number of that length has shrunk to 10%.

Percentage of homes without front and back gardens

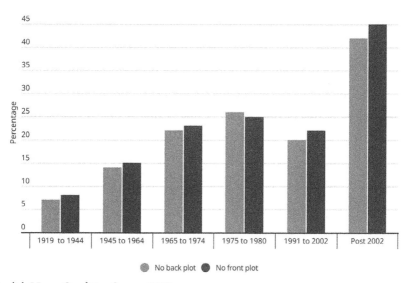

Legend: ● No back plot ● No front plot

English House Condition Survey 2018

The coronavirus lockdown drew attention to the lack of garden space. In May 2020 the Office for National Statistics reported that one in eight households have no access to a garden. In London, the number rises to one in five. Worse, only 8% of those over 65 in London had access to any kind of outdoor space. The ONS also discovered that people from black and ethnic minority groups were four times more likely to have no access to outdoor space, either in their garden, patio, balcony, or shared outside space.

Parking squeeze

The Great Squeeze was tightened by planning guidance issued in 2001 which reversed the way designers are supposed to calculate the number of parking spots. From 'you decide how many the development needs' to 'you can't put more than 1.5 spaces per house into the plans, oh no!' This 'we know what's good for you' approach has reigned ever since. Disputes over parking have blazed ever since. Nowhere more than in Kent. Complaints by residents led to Kent County Council monitoring parking on 401 developments built since 2001. 'The highways department visited sites at specific times to see where people parked,' says David Birkbeck, who was involved in a deeper study of six Kent developments. Even with an average of just over two parking spots per household, 75% of residents said they were unhappy.

'The drawings show where people were supposed to park,' says Birkbeck. 'The pictures which show you where they actually park say it all. These estates were surveyed early on a Saturday morning – the peak period during the week for parking tensions.

'All but one of the case studies found cars parked where they shouldn't be: on pavements, verges, front garden lawns and landscape areas. Eight out of ten people felt that there was inadequate parking, 63% felt that this had led to neighbour disputes,' says Birkbeck, who advises volume builders on design issues. He suggests that the 'we know best' parking advice from planners cuts no ice with owners.

'Only a quarter of people said that lack of parking would put them off from owning a car. Virtually no one agreed with the statement that they would get rid of their car if public transport were improved. The discussion about parking was vociferous, emotive and the opinions expressed were unanimous. There was almost a sense of people having been tricked since the parking problems only became apparent once the scheme was completed. None of the participants could understand how the designers had got things so terribly wrong.'

Birkbeck says the number of allocated spaces should match the average level of car ownership – one space for one- and two-bed units, one to two spaces for three-bed units and two spaces for four-bed larger units. The number of unallocated spaces should at least be 20% in addition to the allocated spaces.'

Homes study

One of the six case studies was of a Bellway cul-de-sac development of thirty-two homes in Edelin Road, Bearsted, a moderately prosperous suburb of Maidstone finished just before the 2008 crash. Here is what the researchers found in 2013.

'The on-street parking spaces on the bend are marked with house numbers. There were forty-four cars parked on the estate at the time of our visit, just under half of which were not in allocated spaces. These cars did make the estate feel congested and made manoeuvring difficult. The road on the bend does not have a pavement, meaning that cars are parked partly on the verges, causing damage and meaning that residents need to walk in the roadway.' Not much different in 2020.

Edelin Road, Saturday morning, March 2020

Parklands, Maidstone

Not much catches the eye examining the planning documents of the Persimmon Parklands development in Maidstone, which lies a few minutes' drive from Edelin Road. There is nothing unremarkable about the development. Hundreds of similar schemes stand all over Britain. The 2.1 hectares of land wraps itself around the Maidstone Studios complex built in the early 1980s to house the long-defunct TV channel TVS. The 2014 application shows seventy-seven units of the type and size listed below. The density is calculated at 35.48 to the hectare. The application lists 154 car park spaces, 134 allocated and twenty unallocated. Sounds quite enough, doesn't it? The home sizes pass without comment from planners.

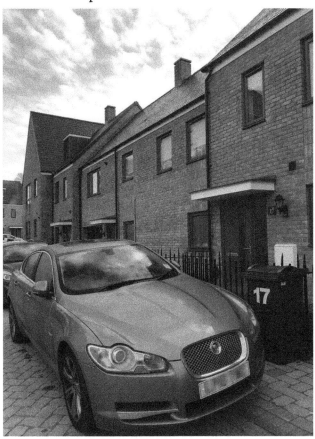

Parklands Maidstone: schedule of home's sizes

Planning Committee Report

2no	1Bed Flat	48.5sqm
14no	2Bed Flat	67.8sqm
7no	2Bed FOGs (flat over garage)	70.2sqm
10no	3Bed +room in the attic (F dormer &R roof light)	68.6sqm
2no	2Bed House	59.3sqm
24no	3Bed House	75.3sqm
4no	3Bed House	83 .0sqm
2no	3Bed House	91.6sqm
8no	3Bed House	92.8sqm
2no	4Bed House	110.2sqm
2no	4Bed House	113.5sqm

The proposal would result in a development with a density of 35.48 dwelling per hectare.

Source: MBC planning application

But look what's been quietly lost. 'For a development of this size, we would expect a minimum on-site provision of open space of 1.00 hectare,' said the Parks Committee. 'We would query whether the proposed provision of open space would meet the minimum expectation of 1.00 hectare, as nearly half the site would need to be in the form of open space,' they say, before helpfully suggesting a monetary solution. 'For every 0.01-hectare shortfall, we would request £15.75 per dwelling. Should the development provide 0.2-hectare on-site open space then we would request a contribution to cover the 0.80-hectare shortfall: 80 x £15.75 = £1,260 per dwelling, which would equate to £97,020 for the development as a whole. Any off-site contribution to be used within a one-mile radius for the improvement of existing areas of open space.' Hands up. Who knew developers can 'off-site' open spaces?

Outside

This is no doubt why barely a blade of grass can be seen when you walk around the estate, which is as well, as the hard surfaces, including pavements, were littered with cars on a Saturday morning in March

2020. Yet there are 154 car park spaces, more than two per dwelling. Planning guidance says that should be ample. What is going on? The garages look unused. The 'carports' were mostly empty. A small boat was parked in one. Big cars, small garages? Small homes, nowhere to put stuff, except in the garages? Maybe. If you can mount the pavement to park just outside the front door, why not?

Three-storey trick

The non-obligatory Nationally Described Space Standards (NDSS) ask for three-storey three-bed homes to range from ninety metres square for a four-person home to 108 metres square for a unit designed for six. Ten of the forty-eight three-bed units in the Parklands original application are over the ninety metres square minimum. The other thirty-eight ranged in size from sixty-nine metres square to eighty-three metres square. In 2017 the application was amended to allow thirteen of the three-bed units to rise a half metre in height to allow an extra bedroom to be popped on top – and to allow Persimmon to add £60,000 to the price.

Three-floor units are now widespread, excused by planners for increasing density and welcomed by developers for increasing profits. But three-floor units reduce the ratio of 'day-time' space to 'night-time' space from 50:50 to roughly 37:63. Not something that seems to concern planners, architects or those who designed the NDSS tables. The second impact of stacking minimum space standards over three floors means the width can be squeezed and, with that, the width of the garden. Sticking with the Imperial measurements shown on the Persimmon plans you can see the width of the semi is eleven feet ten inches, the terrace twelve feet two inches. The narrowest 'home fit for heroes' designed by Tudor Walters was sixteen feet wide. Most were twenty-two feet wide.

PARKLANDS THREE-STOREY SEMI-DETACHED

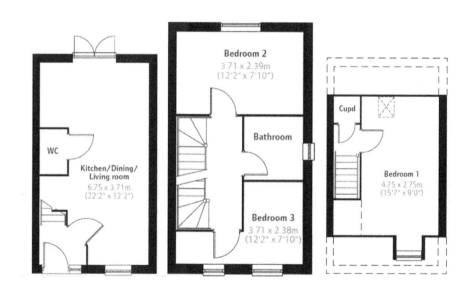

PARKLANDS THREE-STOREY TERRACE

Homes England

The government's 'housing accelerator', Homes England, has its criteria for homes they fund, generally in areas where prices are more than six times the average income. Tenderers have to present pictorial evidence that their designs are in line with the 'good practice' photographs in the document. Not only that, but an enforcement team also makes sure that what is on the final approved drawings gets built. Until that box is ticked, the freehold is withheld. A commendable effort. But there are quite literally no people in the twenty-page picture book Tender Form 5. There are zero cars in most pictures and about as many as you would see in 1955 in others.

Density is lauded with advice that 'bookend' short runs of linked properties are a widely used successful device for *raising* densities. There are no mandatory minimum space standards. The majority of the photographs are small-sized, high-density developments, some with pavements, some with front doors opening directly onto the tarmac. There are no photographs of back gardens.

Beauty parade

The word 'beauty' floated like a butterfly into the housing lexicon in 2018. That November, Communities Secretary James Brokenshire set up the alliterative Building Better, Building Beautiful Commission. A right-of-centre think tank, Policy Exchange, had been preparing the ground with a series of seminars on the topic, led by Jack Airey, head of housing research at Policy Exchange. He went on to join the government in early 2020 as an advisor to Boris Johnson.

Brokenshire served as Theresa May's last Housing Secretary, between April 2018 and July 2019. A neat, bright, impressive politician, I thought, listening to him expound the virtues of beauty at one of those seminars. He had at least changed the narrative from a drive for numbers to something a bit deeper. Something that might quieten the NIMBYs. Five commissioners were appointed under the chairmanship of Sir Roger Scruton, who died not long before the 178-page 'Living with Beauty' report was published in February 2020.

The other commissioners included Adrian Penfold, head of planning at commercial developer British Land and Nicholas Boys Smith, founding director of Create Streets, which was set up to 'promote *high density* [my italics], beautiful, street-based developments'. Specialist advisors included the Master of Emmanuel College Cambridge, Dame Fiona Reynolds; Ben Bolgar, director of the Prince's Foundation and the former head of residential research at Savills; Yolande Barnes, now professor of real estate at University College, London. A couple of quietly distinguished architects, Sunand Prasad and Paul Monaghan, advised. As did housebuilder Stephen Stone, who trained as an architect before building up Crest Nicholson.

A total of forty-five recommendations were made. Boris Johnson's Housing Secretary, Robert Jenrick, promised to take the ideas seriously. Those ideas that might be given weight include national design codes. Imposed on local authorities – unless they draw up their own.

'These local codes should be living documents, able gradually to evolve, informed by ongoing engagement with residents on local preferences and desires,' says the report. 'These form-based codes are a set of illustrated design rules and requirements which instruct on the physical development of a site or area. There are now over 400 form-based codes in US and Canadian cities.'

Larger scale developments would be subject to 'design review – in which planning authorities ask a panel of independent specialists to review a proposed development on its merits'. Easy to say. Hard to find independent experts. The Commission for Architecture and the Built Environment was supposed to fulfil that role – before it was shut down.

The report does tackle the 'well, how much will all this cost?' question. Knight Frank's 'Cost and Value' addendum report covered at the end of Chapter Two underpins the findings: build better and the uplift in prices outmatches the rise in costs.

'The principal objection that will be raised to our proposals is that taking beauty seriously will raise the cost of the product and will, therefore, reduce the supply of affordable housing. In reply we argue as follows: beauty is not necessarily costly. Joined-up terraces, proper squares and green spaces might cost a little, but people might also be prepared to pay for it. Tower blocks in cleared spaces do not necessarily achieve greater density than the terraced streets that they replace.'

A thought that gave birth to the phrase 'Gentle Density'.

Gentle density

Gentle density means 'you can still pack 'em in – but, please, not too high'. As Nicholas Boys Smith admits, his organisation, Create Streets, was set up to promote 'high-density' streets. Better than tower blocks, certainly. But there is a price: the commissioners recommend 'strongly encouraging councils not to impose minimum back-to-back or front-to-front distance between habitable room requirements, which make it impossible to build more finely grained settlements. It should also be made more explicit that councils do not use daylight and sunlight regulations to make it impossible to build more finely grained and popular traditional settlements.' Why more 'finely grained' equates with 'popular' is not explained.

Even so, there is a feeling the recommendations will percolate into the minds of planners and embarrass housebuilders to include the word 'beauty' into their brochures. Boyes Smith says, 'The links between design (and process) with good wellbeing outcomes, value, sustainable land use patterns and greater support for new developments are far (far) more predictable than most designers or architects like to admit.'

Mark Prisk is broadly supportive. 'The report has got some recommendations that are a bit esoteric. But I think the notion of providing homes that people actually want to live in and having respect for the natural vernacular design is a good thing. Very often the housing protests that I encountered as a minister came from people who weren't entirely thrilled that development was happening. But they were particularly hacked off because the developer was building something that looked like it had just dropped down from space and had no respect for the local vernacular design.'

Former Shadow Housing Secretary John Healey is unimpressed. 'I think this is entirely window-dressing. There was a little bit of a mood amongst Tory MPs and Tory circles that somehow homes needed to be better. And this was an exercise in policy PR, rather than anything that was either directed to meeting some of the fundamental elements of the housing crisis.'

Unimpressed housebuilders

Housebuilders are not impressed either. Redrow executive chairman John Tutte condemned the report in *Building* magazine a few days after it was published. 'It's very narrow in what it covers. The examples they give are one-off, bespoke schemes which are very difficult to build and very expensive. It patronises customers. I don't rate the report at all.' The subtext of Tutte's condemnation was this: 'I'm not interested in what the metropolitan elite have to say. We build homes for our customers. We know what they like. That's what we build.' A view that most volume housebuilders share.

Redrow master planning director Kevin Parker explains. 'As it is our customers who will live in the new homes, it is their view of what is attractive and desirable that matters most. Research shows that there continues to be a preference for traditional styles of architecture when choosing a new home. We find a particular fondness for detached homes that are inspired by Arts and Crafts architecture, but with modern interiors designed for today's lifestyles. Together, these features provide for a sense of homeliness and cosiness as well as a functional place to live with a garden, garage and driveway and a bit of privacy.'

Sin of omission

The real sin in attempting to raise design standards is that of omission. The Ghost family played little part in the thinking. There seems to be scant consideration of the hopes and desires of occupants. No request for research into the way we live today. The commission could have quantified one aspect of beauty – space. But there are no recommendations on raising minimum space standards, nor lowering density levels. No Tudor Walters-style measurements on terrace lengths or home widths. Why not? 'The government is terrified of the reaction of housebuilders,' said a Whitehall source.

There is a lot right with the 'Living with Beauty' report. 'How did we go from this [pre- WW11] to the creation of the soulless mono-tenure estates that blight their residents' lives?' is a very good question. But the answers tend to patronise the occupiers.

- Residents need to be encouraged to walk, and (told of) the corresponding benefits to the environment by removing the need to drive.
- Residents would be required to agree to a design code, so each of them could have confidence that any changes their neighbours might make would harmonise.
- Milton Keynes covers an area twice the size of Florence but contains half as many residents. We don't have spare land to play with, in that car-dependent way. Some kind of 'gentle density' is what we must aim to achieve.

Cram or be damned

As things stand, cramming is actively encouraged. What follows is taken from the 2019 National Planning Policy Framework, the guide used by all councils when determining planning applications. The conclusions are chilling: if you don't cram, you may not get permission. Unit numbers matter, people don't count for much.

'Where there is an existing or anticipated shortage of land for meeting identified housing needs, it is especially important that planning policies and decisions *avoid homes being built at low densities.*' [My italics]. Yes, you read that right. 'This will be tested robustly at examination and should include the use of minimum density standards for city and town centres. These standards should seek a significant uplift in the average density of residential development. Planning authorities should refuse applications which they consider fail to make efficient use of land.'

Tudor Walters would turn in his grave at the next homily. 'When considering applications for housing, authorities should take a flexible approach in applying policies or guidance relating to daylight and sunlight.' Who cares if the Ghost family live in semi-darkness and the hamster dies for lack of air? The NPPG then do what newspaper folk call 'a reverse ferret'. 'Good design is a key aspect of sustainable development, creates better places in which to live and work, and helps make the development acceptable to communities.'

Poor experiment

Academics from the Royal Holloway, Goldsmiths and Oxford Brookes universities spoke to the residents of an acclaimed development in Lewisham in the summer of 2019. The twenty-four flats designed by Rogers Stirk + Harbour were occupied in 2016. A flat-pack design was chosen for the 'pop-up' development. The two-bed open-plan white-walled flats were designed to hold a family of four. The occupants housed were those teetering on the edge of homelessness, families who had been moved from pillar to post.

The high ceilings and natural light were welcomed. 'It made us feel really special,' said one resident. 'This one actually feels like a home. We've got our room, the kids got their room, there's enough space for the kids to run about, there ain't a garden but there's a balcony, we've got a big enough bathroom, we ain't sharing it, got our own toilet, it does feel like home… for the time being.' An end-note of anxiety, as the flats are not meant to be permanent. Even so, 'Being able to live in something of this quality makes you want to earn, makes you want something in life. I want a house with a garden... a little swing and a paddling pool, have people around. It's given us just that little taste of life... and yeah, a bit of hope.'

The bad news? 'Residents are forbidden from hanging anything on the white walls. The large-windowed flats are too hot in summer. The radiators too hot in winter. There is scorn for the cycle racks – 'we need somewhere to park!' The high prices in the café downstairs: '£7.20 for a poached egg on toast. I can't afford that!' The researchers found the bold design 'may also have bolstered a sense we found among residents of feeling like guinea pigs. The residents experienced anxiety deriving from a suspicion that the primary purpose of the building was not to house them but to showcase the building to others.'

I drive past the development regularly. The drab reality is a long way from the bright Computer Generated Images. Traffic roars by. There is little privacy through the picture windows. By 2020, the cladding was grimed and dulled by traffic muck. The place looks garish, grubby. To repeat what one tenant said, '...I want a house with a garden... a little swing and a paddling pool, have people around.'

FIVE

LAND FOR HOPE AND GLORY

'This land is your land; this land is my land… this land was made for you and me.'

Woody Guthrie

How to apportion the increase in land value conferred by the state granting permission to build homes? A topic debated since at least 1879, when American economist Henry George proposed taxes on income and suggested profits be scrapped in favour of a single tax on land. Three years before his death, in 1897, *The Single Tax* magazine was launched, a title published to this day, now under the spangled banner *Land&Liberty*. Henry George is not forgotten. His foundation thrives, lobbying globally for land taxes. In 1928, George Bernard Shaw said, 'single taxers are not wrong in principle, but they are behind the times.' Ahead, more like. Since 1909, attempts to redistribute land value uplifts have been tried, failed, tried again, undermined by a push-me, pull-you struggle between the left, who want to tax more, and the right, who want to tax less.

A global campaign to capture land value was launched in 2018 by the US-based Lincoln Institute. Founder John Lincoln (no relation to Abe) was an inventor, bitten by the Georgist bug. He set up his institution in 1946 at the age of eighty, along with his son David, who died in 2018.

'Land value capture is based on a simple premise – public action should generate public benefit,' says Mac McCarthy, CEO of the Lincoln Institute. 'On every continent, communities already deploy forms of land value capture, the most common include: betterment contributions, business improvement districts, inclusionary housing, linkage or impact fees, public land leasing, special assessments, transferable development rights. However, these practices face persistent barriers to adoption, including the lack of local capacity, and inadequate access to practical knowledge.'

The Liberal Party's Housing and Town Planning Act of 1909 fixed a 50% betterment levy on any increase in value. This badly drafted provision had more holes that a Connect 4 board. It was paid on just three occasions, according to a detailed history from planning barrister Richard Bacon QC. The Town and Country Planning Act 1932 had a provision for a 75% betterment levy – and even better ways of avoiding the tax. By 1942, not a single penny had been collected.

In 2004, Wyndham Thomas, then Vice-President of the Town and Country Planning Association, wrote an instructive essay on the history of land taxes between 1947 and 1997 for the Smith Institute think tank. Thomas was personally involved in many of the initiatives and knew many of the actors. He died, aged, ninety-five, in early 2020. What follows is an edited version from the man who was there:

Wyndham Thomas

'There have been three failed attempts since WWII to introduce a system for taxing the increased value of land conferred by the granting of planning permission: the 1947 Planning Act's development charge, the 1967 Land Commission Act's betterment levy and the Development Land Tax Act of 1976, which complemented the 1975 Community Land Act. Each attempt failed because no practicable system for collecting "betterment" can be devised.'

1945–51 Labour

'An expert committee was set up in 1941 by the wartime coalition government under Mr Justice Uthwatt. He suggested that since the owner had contributed nothing to the betterment, it belonged logically to the public at large, something the incoming Labour government thought a very fine judgement indeed. Labour's Town and Country Planning Act of 1947 nationalised all development rights. An owner would have to pay to the Central Land Board – a new agency – a development charge, fixed in 1948 at 100% of the difference between the land's existing use value and its permitted use-value. Except for public authorities; they would buy land at existing use value. To prevent development seizing up a £300 million compensation fund was set up.'

1951–64 Conservatives

'Happily, for developers, the Conservatives won the 1951 election. The 1953 Planning Act provided that each admitted claim would be paid out only when an owner was refused permission. Not many obtained planning consents and then sold on for private development. So, the total eventually paid out was well short of the £300 million.

'Conservative Chancellor, Rab Butler, wanted to keep the development charge, but at 70% or even 60%. But Housing Minister Harold Macmillan wanted the charge abolished. Macmillan won in Cabinet, and his 1954 Planning Act abolished the development charge. That lead to anger among landowners still forced to sell to the state at exiting use-value. Opposition was led by the National Farmers' Union, the Law Society and the RICS. They all said they wanted "equal justice". What they meant was a lot more money.

'With Macmillan as Prime Minister, the 1959 Town and Country Planning Act gave them everything. The simple purpose was to restore "current market value" as the price for the publicly acquired land. But what is the current market value of land for schools, hospitals or roads? Some devilishly ingenious civil servant conjured up the notion of a certificate of alternative development. What other development might have been permitted under some other fictional plan? Down the years, the criterion of nearest prevailing use has come to be applied. This ill-contrived and loosely worded compensation code has caused prolonged disputation and a huge overload of work, especially for the local planning authorities, the Land Tribunal and the high courts.

'The 1959 Act led to a surge in land values – and an abrupt end to the National Farmers' Union's claims that every acre of farmland taken for public projects was precious beyond price to keep the nation fed. Owners of land allocated for development were now in an enviable position, gathering in large and rising capital gains, free of tax. The speculative pursuit of planning consents became a rewarding pastime, as the planning system distributed fortunes with all the inconsequence of a fruit machine.'

1964–71 Labour

'The Labour Party proposed a Land Commission with powers to buy all land coming forward for development before the 1964 election. After Labour won the Treasury had to help produce something practicable; but now in association with a new Ministry of Land and Natural Resources – a capricious and pointless Harold Wilson invention. So, it was not until 1967 that the Land Commission Act was passed. Sir Henry Wells was the commission's chairman [Wyndham Thomas was a member].

'The Land Commission had three main purposes. To collect a "betterment" levy, set at 40%, with the promise or threat of 45% and then 50%. The second purpose was to buy land allocated for housing in local development plans. The third purpose was to reduce the cost of land for public purposes by providing that public agencies would buy net of the betterment levy. The Conservative opposition's reaction was immediate: "We'll abolish the Land

Commission." In consequence, a civil service trawl failed to attract the quality of staff. Stringent accounting rules were imposed by the Treasury. There was resentment from Housing Minister Richard Crossman and Evelyn Sharp, his Permanent Secretary, that the commission was not under the planning ministry's control.'

1971–73 Conservatives

'The Conservatives won the 1970 election and at once set about winding up the commission. By then it had bought 2,800 acres of land, with another 9,000 acres in the pipeline. In the early 1970s, another property boom had gained pace. Shortages of building land became more acute, and commercial property values in London and the South East in particular soared. Newspapers criticised the Heath government's failure either to hold down commercial property prices or rents. The result was ministerial panic. Its outcome was Edward Heath's 1973 development gains tax. Development land gains had earlier been subject to capital gains tax at 30%. The new development gains tax proposed to treat these gains as income and to tax them progressively.'

1974–79 Labour

'But then came the three-day working week and two general elections in 1974, which put Labour back into office. Labour restated its intention to work towards the public ownership of all development land and to recoup all development values. This lamentable regression was due to Labour's Planning Minister, John Silkin. The outcome was the Community Land Act of 1975 and the Development Land Tax Act of 1976. Silkin said his was a ten-year programme of three stages. In stage one, local authorities were empowered to buy any building land. In stage two, they would be compelled to do so by ministerial order. In stage three, all development and redevelopment land would be taken into public ownership as it came forward for development; but then at a new base value, which might only be *existing use value. The community land scheme was grandiose and impracticable, far beyond its competence to deliver.'*

1979–97 Conservatives

'Margaret Thatcher's 1979 government repealed the Community Land Act. But a development land tax was retained and reduced to 60%. Any euphoria over the retention of development land tax was short-lived. In 1985 Chancellor Nigel Lawson abolished it. It was, he said, costing much more to collect than other taxation; and henceforth capital gains tax at 40% would take care of development land value gains.

'In the vacuum created by the abolition of development land tax, more alert planning authorities saw an opportunity to seek contributions from developers towards the cost of their services and other public projects. The result has been the fitful evolution of what came to be called planning gain. The negotiation of these agreements, especially for large developments, is usually complicated, often disputatious and always prolonged. The system is acknowledged to be hugely expensive for all concerned and a major cause of project delays. And the large extra costs fall, as always, on those who buy or rent the finished buildings. If there were no other reason for the introduction of a development gains tax, there is reason enough in the urgent need to replace the planning gain system.'

Building Sustainable Communities, *Smith Institute*, November 2004

Community infrastructure levy

Tony Blair wasn't the least interested in housing or taxing land. Housing he left to his Deputy, John Prescott; taxes he left to his Chancellor, Gordon Brown – the latter keeping a close eye on the former. It took a few years before Brown turned his attention to the taxing land value uplifts. Between 1997 and 2000, the Chancellor had been busy quadrupling stamp duty on property transactions from 1% to 4%. Brown knew his history and was, by nature, a cautious man. So, he began to ask for studies to be done, notably by Bank of England economist Kate Barker. The one I got involved with was conducted by the Smith Institute in 2004. The Institute was run by the Chancellor's friend and confidante, Wilf Stevenson, given a peerage in Brown's 2010 resignation honour's list.

I was editor of *Estates Gazette* in 2004. Stevenson asked if I could edit a series of essays for the Institute on land value capture. We called the publication, 'Sustainable communities: capturing land development value for the public realm'. The subtitle of the booklet (which contained the Wyndham Thomas essay) was, of course, the real title.

Kate Barker argued in her essay for the introduction of a planning gain supplement (PGS). Yet another 'betterment' levy. Ex-Tory Environment Secretary, John Gummer, argued against a PGS on philosophical grounds: 'A betterment tax is wrong in principle and like most things that are fundamentally wrong, it will always fail in practice. Property must not be stolen from its rightful owners, even by men of goodwill with the best of intentions.'

No 11 meeting

On November 3rd 2004, about 150 senior civil servants and various housing experts gathered in the chilly, bare-boarded upstairs room at No 11 Downing Street at 8.30 am. The way these things work is, the report's editor gets to make the introductory speech. Kate Barker had published the first of her reports on solving Britain's housing crisis that spring. Her PGS proposal was on the agenda.

I no longer have my speech. But it began with a rant that went something like this: 'For crying out loud! You can't tax an opinion. What one valuer will say is worth X, another will say is worth 80% of X or 120% of X, if it suits. You have seen how Labour has screwed this up time and again. Don't screw up again. If you even want to think about taxing development gains, you have to do it based on actual transaction figures. Even then it will be a nightmare.'

Barker had also recommended the reining back and simplification of the section 106 regime, by altering it to a tariff. This inevitably led to the invention of yet another tax, the Community Infrastructure Levy, *and* the retention of section 106 taxes. Liz Peace was chief executive of the British Property Federation at the time, so close to the thinking of the Blair government. Back in 2013, the former senior civil servant traced the genesis of CIL in *Planet Property*:

'[Kate Barker's] review came out in March 2004. Out of the document came the idea that we might have what they called a planning gain supplement or PGS. Barker had particularly focused on landowners who made a huge amount of money out of the grant of planning permission for new homes. The property industry decided to come up with alternative proposals to minimise the damaging effects of the planned legislation. The key issue was to get the industry bodies to coalesce around one way of doing it. Sir Stuart Lipton helped bring together housebuilders and developers to agree a tariff system which applied a fixed sum per square metre of development.'

CIL-born

The Treasury eventually agreed to a tariff-based tax. The Community Infrastructure Levy was conceived. Gestation took years. The levy was introduced in April 2010. The Conservatives had opposed the idea while in opposition, objections which quietly dissolved after the coalition government was formed in summer 2010. It took until April 2011 for the complex regulations to be published. The idea appeared simple enough: a fixed charge per square metre determined by the local council. Typically, £50 to £100, the chargeable space being the extra square metres created by the development. In practice, CIL metastasised into a monster of complexity'.

Peace continues: 'After a year or so, the property sector was getting fed up with the tax. Robert Noel was chief executive of Landsec. Rob rang me to tell me he was going to be seeing [Secretary of State] Eric Pickles.

He asked me what he should say about CIL. So, I gave him some bullets and he, in his inimitable blunt way, fired them with force. The phone rang within twenty-four hours summoning us to a meeting. We got Pickles to listen. He ordered his junior, Nick Boles, to sort things out. We started well, with fixes for things like payment in kind, exemptions for large complex sites. But then officials decided it was necessary to listen to all those who did not want radical solutions. We ended up with just another set of tweaks to the system that didn't make any difference at all.'

By 2016, the CIL regulations were 155 pages long and consisted of 129 separate regulations. They had been amended each year since 2010 to cope with technical screw-ups, block loopholes, grant exemptions and enact policy changes. In 2016, Peace, by then chair of the Government Property Agency, was asked to conduct an inquiry into the tax by the Conservative government.

'The overall complexity has led to a system which is difficult to understand, expensive to operate and uncertain in its implementation,' says Peace. 'There was almost universal agreement that the regulations should be made simpler.' Liz Peace suggested a simpler path in her report which was published in 2017. 'We propose a twin-track system of a new Local Infrastructure Tariff (LIT), combined with Section 106 for larger sites, that captures the best of both worlds, optimises the contributions from those smaller sites which may not otherwise be contributing in a Section 106 system and also ensures the more substantial infrastructure needs of larger developments.

'The LIT should be applied to all developments, almost without exception,' said Peace. 'If it is set at a sufficiently low level we do not consider that this will lead to difficulties or indeed a widespread call for exemptions or relief.' The government pushed Peace's plan into a pigeon hole, for later consideration, it turned out. In August 2020 the government proposed scrapping CIL and Section 106 payments and replacing both with an 'infrastructure tax.' A tax payable only when the homes are occupied, killing the need to make guesses about value.

Trying to capture land value, again

A year-long parliamentary investigation concluded in September 2018 that a way to capture land value must be found, despite a century of failure. The Housing, Communities and Local Government Committee, chaired by Clive Betts MP, took testimony from over 100 sources, both for and against the tax. Select committee members included Conservative MP Kevin Hollinrake, who forged the Hunters chain of estate agents, and former Housing Minister Mark Prisk. Witnesses included Philip Barnes, Group Land Director at Barratt. Conclusions were reached: 'when considering new mechanisms, it is vital that we learn the lessons from the past. Any new approach should have cross-party support... and should be simple to administer, without complicated exceptions or viability processes. It will also need to allocate land value increases fairly between central government, local authorities and landowners, without undermining incentives to sell or risk holding up the development process.'

The Betts Committee also said: 'We believe that the Land Compensation Act 1961 requires reform so that local authorities have the power to compulsorily purchase land at a fairer price. The present right of landowners to receive "hope value" serves to distort land prices, encourage land speculation, and reduce revenues for affordable housing, infrastructure and local services. Reform will provide a powerful tool for local authorities to build a new generation of new towns, as well as extensions to, or significant developments within, existing settlements.' Mark Prisk recalls the discussions. 'The select committee came up with a reasonably practical set of proposals,' he says. 'But, history is of governments trying to get hold of a jelly. Nothing works.' But perhaps there is another, more subtle way.

Letwin Report

In October 2018, then Conservative MP Sir Oliver Letwin produced a well-received proposal to capture land value – just on land capable of holding more than 1,500 units. The former Tory mandarin also produced ideas to manage these large-scale settlements (Chapter Six). The key, said Sir Oliver, was to allow local planning authorities to zone parcels of land for housing. Then: 'be given clear statutory powers to purchase the land compulsorily at prices which reflect the value once they have planning permission for a masterplan that reflects the new diversity requirements to the point where they generate a maximum residual development value for the land of around ten times existing use value rather than the huge multiples of existing use value which currently apply.'

Put more simply: the planning authority pinpoints the land and determines what gets built before granting permission. This allows them to add in 'value' in the form of fewer, bigger homes, and/or increase the number of affordable homes, Section 106 contributions in kind, such as schools and community centres. Right up to the point where the residual land value is depressed from, say, fifty times its value as housing land to no more than ten times the existing use value. Give that ten-fold increase to the landowner.

The interesting thing about Oliver Letwin's proposals is, they did get past the Treasury, says Lord Barwell, the Prime Minister's Chief of Staff at the time. 'The Chancellor endorsed his idea. But then it got slowed up in the implementation. I'm not sure if the Treasury was fighting a rear-guard action, having signed up to it in principle, or, whether it was a capacity issue in CLG. Grenfell then imposed this huge additional burden. Resources were inevitably shifted from working on reforming the market, building more homes, to places where people are currently living, making them safe places to live.'

Off into the long grass

Housing and Communities Secretary James Brokenshire duly pigeon-holed the Letwin proposal, remarking 'new planning guidance' would be sufficient. The Conservatives came closer to sorting out an equitable split in land value increases than generally realised. In Liam Halligan's excellent 2019 book, *Home Truths*, Chancellor Sajid Javid discloses he researched reforms in 2016/17 when Housing and Communities Secretary. 'We worked on a 50:50 split between landowners and local government. This would be an efficient and morally justifiable tax. The state is expected to create the infrastructure around new housing and that needs to be paid for: so, a 50:50 makes sense.'

Former Shadow Housing Secretary John Healey praises Sir Oliver. 'He went about it in a very serious way. He made up his mind and gathered his evidence and conducted his conversations about this. He was hamstrung in the end by having to produce something that he felt was sufficiently finely tuned to find acceptability by a Conservative government when essentially the diagnosis of the problem leads you to a conclusion that action is required, which is fundamentally un-Conservative.' Labour policy is to create a state land-buying body, akin to the Central Land Board of 1947. 'We've proposed an English Sovereign Land Trust,' says Healey of the proposal in Labour's 2019 manifesto, 'Housing for the Many'. 'That would have powers, alongside local councils' ability to purchase land at nearer current-use value. So, it would involve some amendment of the 1961 Act.'

Change the 1961 Act

Toby Lloyd was the housing policy advisor in 10 Downing Street at the time. 'I wholly support and campaign for changing the 1961 Act. But it's not about changing it to existing use value; it's about changing the definition of market value. Sounds like a minor thing, but it's critical. As soon as you start saying you can't pay people market value there are very significant human rights objections, quite rightly so.

'If you're going to take someone's property off them, you need to give them the market value,' Lloyd says. 'Everything hangs on the definition of market value. In any rational world, the market value would reflect all of the things you're going to expect that land to have to do. Not just the fact that in theory, some bigger idiot might've turned up with a fat cheque at some point in the future. But that's what we're talking about – it's not about existing use value; it's about real market value.

What you need to do is to lower the value of the land. CPOs are there to suppress land values. But it has to be a credible threat.

'Changing the 1961 Act is critical. But doing that alone, won't mean anything. You then need to have proactive intervention to use that power, or at least deliver the credible threat to use it. You need a public body, or at least a public-interested body. It doesn't have to be in the public sector; we've got fantastic places that have been built by our aristocratic landowners, charities, private companies. It does not matter as long as they have the public interest as their motivation, primarily.

'You still make a profit, but it has to be public, and it has to have a long-term view. And that could be, like a Letchworth, which was built by a voluntary coming together of a bunch of hippies and vegetarians and Quakers. Fine. Poundbury was built by Prince Charles because he owned the land and he could. It doesn't matter who it is, as long as you've got those characteristics. Once you get the land at a cheap price then you can get long-term money.'

Former Housing Minister Lord Barwell lost his marginal seat in the June 2017 election. He has no doubts about his agenda if he had stayed as Housing Minister instead of moving to No 10 to run the Prime Minister's office. 'The one thing I would want to be pushing ahead with very aggressively would be land reform, to ensure that we are buying at a price that allowed us to develop homes that are affordable for people to buy and to rent.'

Land for hope and (my) glory

I decided to solve the housing crisis in the autumn of 2018. At least there was a very powerful incentive to pretend to do so: £50,000. The prize money was offered by the right-of-centre Institute of Economic Affairs. I lost, happily able to blame the judge, Jacob Rees-Mogg, a derided figure among us Remainers during the Brexit Crisis. I could scorn the young winner who suggested giving plots of land to the people to build their own home. Very Ayn Rand. My plan was lifted from the shoulders of others: the state should capture land value through stronger CPO powers. The only thing new was that the money should be used to build half market rent homes, or what the housing association world calls 'social rents'.

The 3,000-word essay entitled 'Land for Hope and Glory' suggested that renting out 'affordable' homes at 80% of the market rent makes them unaffordable for 80% of those seeking accommodation. Here is my summary, including ideas for right and left. No point in suggesting anything that appeals to one party and not the other.

- ✦ **Act one:** amend Compulsory Purchase Order law to allow authorities to buy land at existing use value on sites zoned for homes to generate land bounty. Use 80% of bounty to fund Half Market Rent (HMR) homes. Councils spend 20% on local improvements. Bounty realised by JV with the private sector or housing associations. Equity in HMR slow-released to the occupant.

- ✦ **Act two:** set an aspirational five-year target of 300,000 new homes a year. Aim for consensus. Accept aim leaves a 70,000 shortfall to be filled by State. Accept downturn will hit the aim. Burgeoning Build to Rent (BTR) sector included in bounty initiative to boost numbers. Embed bounty powers into Urban Development and New Town Corporations to galvanise building programmes and cut public spending.

- ✦ **Orchestration:** decry factoids, such as 'more new homes will lower prices', 'fixing planning will fix crisis', 'prefabrication, hurrah!' Rescore mood music from regretful to rousing. Prime Minister to echo Churchillian message 'build the houses for the people'. Bounty lets more people 'step up' the equity staircase and buy. Bounty bonus – it supercharges the new town's programme.

Added political options

+ Go right: offer the landowner a fixed percentage of the uplift, determined at the time of sale by independent valuer and subject of an appeal. Compress time scale to allow occupants 100% equity in two or three years.

+ Go left: All money goes to pay for council homes rented in perpetuity. Go local: let individual councils decide left/right options.

A set of caveats and elaborations was added, for safety's sake:

+ **Prevent abuse, promote consensus**

   There must be rules to prevent the spoils wrested from the landowner benefitting anyone who speedily sells their home. First, to ensure the idea meets the 'politically possible' test – being acceptable to both main parties. Even the threat of repeal by Labour will kill the idea. Second, to mute uproar from landowners.

+ **A land bounty can turn renters into owners, slowly**

   Equity in units sold to occupants under the government Affordable Home Ownership scheme. Equity released for sale slowly, over ten to fifteen years, to prevent profiteering. Result? 'Slow release' of land bounty to allow stable renters to become stable owners.

+ **Who gets to build HMR homes?**

   Any willing supplier. If the private sector wishes to joint venture with a planning authority which has bought land at existing use value, then, fine. The number of HMR homes built then forms part of the negotiations and subsequent planning obligations. Same goes for deals done with housing associations.

Conclusion

No, that's not likely to work either. Because Plan P. Bill also requires the taxing of an opinion; how much is the land worth? Nothing that has been tried over the last 110 years to capture the uplift in land values has worked. That is why the proposal by the Johnson administration in 2020 to base a tax on transaction values is clever. But, time will tell. Every attempt is wrecked by the inclusion of clauses that demand the taxing of an opinion, rather than a transaction. It gets worse: even when land transactions were taxed under the Capital Gains Tax regime, that didn't work either – and led to a Conservative government under Edward Heath introducing the 1973 Development Gains Tax. As Liz Peace says of her experiences with the Community Land Tax: 'We decided in the endless debates within my CIL Review Group, there is no easy answer – if there was, somebody would have found it.' The hunt for a way to tax land is not over. In fact it has widened to include a tax on existing commercial property. In the summer of 2020 there were reports that the Treasury was considering replacing business rates paid by benighted retailers with a 'land and buildings tax' on landlords. Chancellor, Rishi Sunak was said to be taken with the idea. Those who don't first read the lessons of history Rishi…

SIX

GARDEN PATHS

'You can't trust the private sector to protect the public interest.'
Urban planner Edward Logue

On August 19th 2019, the Prince of Wales made one of his periodic pleas for better design. Twenty-five years after founding Poundbury on the outskirts of Dorchester, the Prince said, 'We must consign the monocultural housing estate to the past and build beautiful, mixed-use, walkable places of which future generations will be proud.' A week later local councillors were complaining that builders were cutting affordable home sizes at his Dorset village by up to 10%. Still, Poundbury remains an obligatory walk-round for designers of garden communities. There are plenty on the stocks.

In 2020, there were fifteen 'garden towns' (over 10,000 homes) and thirty-four 'garden villages' (up to 10,000 homes) designated by government. Planning consultants, Litchfields, estimated these forty-nine 'garden communities' have the capacity for 403,000 homes. They are sprinkled across England, although concentrated in the south as the list and the map on pages 106-107 shows.

Included in the list are twenty-three spots seeded up to a quarter of a century ago. The other twenty-six remain largely un-germinated. Most have only appeared on the official list since August 2018, when the government made a general call for sites wishing to be granted official status, meaning all twenty-six have agreed to abide by a set of guidelines and so qualify as 'garden towns' or 'garden villages'.

Eco-towns to garden communities

Some earlier settlements began life as 'eco-towns'. Each had signed up to the newly fashionable dream of being 'holistically planned, self-sustaining, and characterful', says yellowing official literature from 2007. 'High-quality place-making' is called for and 'including at its heart an attractive and functioning centre and public realm' and 'a wide range of high-quality, distinctive homes'. Tender ideals, which tend to wilt under the glare of development appraisals. Why? Because, 'We do not want to impose a set of development principles,' say the guidelines.

'When I became Housing Minister in June 2009, I had to sort out the dog's dinner that was eco-towns,' remembers John Healey. 'What was clear is that big developers were branding essentially the big planning applications they'd had on their stocks for some years as eco-towns. After 2010, they started becoming garden extensions. Now they are garden villages, garden towns and now, garden communities. I don't really know what garden communities are. The phrase is being used as a green cover for extension of existing settlements, which is just your bog-standard big add-on development.'

Programme concerns

Concern over the whole 'gardens' programme was expressed in late 2019, by planners Litchfields. 'Whilst the garden communities prospectus did provide some criteria for appraising bids, the context, location and forms of development emerging through the programme do not appear to follow a particular template,' said Litchfields. 'This diversity, which reflects that the proposals are locally-led, may not in itself be undesirable. However, it does raise questions of expectation – is there a sufficiently clear understanding of what a "garden community" is intended to represent?

'Garden communities status is not a "golden ticket" to securing an allocation or planning permission,' warn Litchfields. 'Only a third have permission and/or allocation in an adopted plan. Another one third are in emerging plans, and a full 30% are yet to achieve formal planning status. This means two thirds still need to establish the principle of development and are therefore subject to ongoing levels of planning risk. A number of proposals have experienced delay because of insufficient evidence that the schemes are well-conceived or deliverable.' Less politely: a lot of these schemes are rubbish.

Finally, if politicians think garden communities are going to flower during their political lifetime, think again. 'Our modelling suggests the garden communities programme will take until at least 2050 to build out fully,' said Litchfields. 'Based on our assumptions, the programme will deliver only around 21,000 homes by 2024, before increasing for the period from 2025, ramping up to a peak rate of delivery of around 16,000 per annum after 2030 continuing until about 2044 before tapering (to 13,000 dwellings per annum) by the late 2040s.'

It's not all bad news. Garden communities had delivered 14,000 completions by April 2019, calculated Litchfields. There is, of course, a but: 'Where garden communities have already begun to deliver, they have typically comprised extensions to existing settlements. Bicester, Aylesbury and Didcot alone make up around 14% of homes already completed.' Just 390,000 to go as of summer 2020.

NAME	BEGAN	HOMES	NAME	BEGAN	HOMES
North Essex (15)	Dec-15	43,000	Dalton (40)	Jun-19	4,500
North Northants (14)	Mar-16	33,000	South Godstone (38)	Jun-19	4,000
Harlow and Gilston (11)	Jan-17	24,000	Spitalgate Heath (37)	Jan-17	3,700
Exeter (13)	May-19	20,000	Long Marston (35)	Jan-17	3,500
Uttlesford (12)	Mar-19	18,500	Dunton Hills (34)	Jan-17	4,000
Aylesbury (6)	Dec-15	15,000	Bailrigg (33)	Jan-17	3,500
Ebbsfleet	Mar-14	15,000	Whetstone (36)	Jun-19	3,500
Grazely (10)	Jan-17	15,000	Elvington (32)	Jun-19	3,339
Didcot (9)	Jan-17	15,000	Infinity (31)	Jan-17	3,200
Taunton (8)	Mar-19	14,000	Borough Green Gardens (29)	Jun-19	3,000
Bicester (7)	Dec-14	13,000	Cyber Central (30)	Jun-19	3,000
Hemel (5)	Nov-16	11,000	Threemilestone (28)	Jun-19	2,700
St Cuthbert's (48)	Mar-19	10,325	Dunsfold Park (27)	Jun-19	2,600
Tewkesbury (4)	Mar-19	10,195	Burtree (23)	Jun-19	2,310
Basingstoke (1)	Mar-16	10,060	Berinsfield (26)	Jun-19	2,300
Otterpool Park (2)	Jan-17	10,000	St George's B. (25)	Jan-17	2,215
Meecebrook (3)	Mar-19	10,000	Eynsham (24)	Jun-19	2,200
North East Chelmsford (47)	Jun-19	9,850	Longcross (22)	Jan-17	1,718
Chilmington Green (46)	Jun-19	7,250	Handforth (21)	Jan-17	1,650
Dorchester (39)	Jun-19	7,000	Halsnead (20)	Jan-17	1,589
N' Abbot (45)	Jan-17	6,806	West Carclaze (17)	Jan-17	1,500
Welborne (44	Jan-17	6,000	Biggleswade (18)	Jan-17	1,500
Culm (42)	Jun-19	5,000	South Seaham (19)	Jun-19	1,500
Shapley (43)	Jun-19	5,000	Tresham (16)	Jun-19	1,500
Skerningham (41)	Jun-19	4,500	TOTAL		403,000

Source: Litchfields

Distribution of garden communities

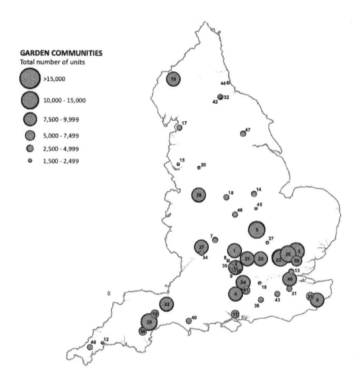

Source: Litchfields

HISTORY

This latest branding deliberately harks back to the 'gardens' movement, which led to Bedford Park in West London in the 1880s, then to Hampstead Garden suburb, set up under an Act of Parliament in 1906, after the purchase of 243 acres of land from Eton College. Hansard writer and founder of the Town and Country Planning Association Sir

Ebenezer Howard set up the Garden Cities Movement, publishing his utopian vision *Garden Cities of Tomorrow* in 1902. The following year, work began on Letchworth Garden City.

In September 1903, six square miles of land outside Hitchin were purchased by 'First Garden City Ltd', an idealistic group of what today would be dismissed as a 'group of *Guardian*-reading, yoghurt-knitting hippies.'

In 1905, the company held the first 'Cheap Cottages Exhibition' to popularise Letchworth. The *Daily Mail* sponsored the event, which eventually morphed into the Ideal Home Exhibition. The original 3,800 acres on which Letchworth was built cost First Garden City £160,000, around £42 an acre, or £5,000 an acre in today's money. Another 880 acres were added later, also at agricultural land prices. Howard suggested that out of a marriage of town and country would spring 'a new hope, a new life, a new civilisation.' He illustrated the idea with his Three Magnets diagram, which put people at the centre of the force field.

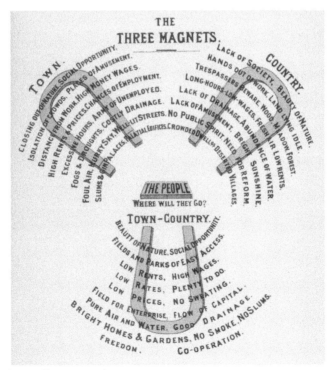

Ebenezer Howard's magnetic plan

Post-war new towns

Welwyn Garden City followed shortly after the First World War. The 1930s Depression stalled progress on others. But new towns bloomed after the Second World War. Ten were designated under the 1946 New Towns Act: Stevenage, Crawley, Hemel Hempstead, Harlow, Newton Aycliffe, Peterlee, Welwyn Garden City and Hatfield, Basildon, Bracknell, and Corby. They were able to take advantage of buying land cheaply – under the threat of Labour's compulsory purchase laws.

The next half-dozen – Skelmersdale, Telford, Redditch, Runcorn and Washington – were in the second wave, along with Milton Keynes. Land values were judged on a 'no scheme world' basis. The land valuation would be on the basis that the new town was not being built. In other words, mostly at agricultural prices. Then the movement wilted and died, seemingly for no good reason. No new towns under the 1946 Act have been designated since 1970.

Consortium developments

In 1983, under Mrs Thatcher, the ten largest housebuilding companies joined forces as Consortium Developments to promote new communities 'initiated and constructed by private enterprise'. They provoked bitter opposition. The purists were quick to point out that they were not really new towns at all, but commuter dormitories. None were constructed after housebuilders lost heart.

Prescott plans

Labour resurrected the state model after Tony Blair came to power. His Chancellor, Gordon Brown, was worried that lack of homes in the South East was hindering economic growth. Deputy Prime Minister John Prescott produced a report in 2002, saying that, 'The New Towns very much reflected best practice at that time. Density levels are too low.' [Yes, too low.] In a clumsy attempt to capture the growing 'save the planet' zeitgeist, Labour rebranded new towns as 'eco-towns'. In 2007, a competition was launched to build ten. Fifteen bids were received. Four were accepted in 2009. One on army land in Hampshire. The second on China clay works in Cornwall. The third on an American Air Force base at Rackheath in Norfolk. The fourth north-west of Bicester in Oxfordshire. A total of 18,500 homes were promised. How are they going ten years on? Slowly, or not at all.

Progress reports

The army didn't leave their Hampshire base until 2015. A few hundred homes have been built at Whitehill and Bordon. A new school opened in late 2019. But plans to build a town centre for the eventual 3,350 homes were only submitted in early 2019. The plan now? To transform the town from 'garrison town to green, healthy and connected town' – by 2036. The 5,000-unit Cornish clay-pit eco-town? Still on the drawing board in 2019. Plans for a 1,500-home 'garden village' and the school have been approved. Plans to build the centre of the village were submitted in late 2019. Rackheath? Now also a 'garden village'. A masterplan for 4,000 homes was endorsed in 2018. Bitter fights with locals over ten years and Barratt's resistance to building more than 10% 'affordable' homes have delayed the plans for a decade. Barratt says a 293-hectare development is not viable if they build more than one in ten of the homes for poorer folk. They now plan to build just 500 homes. Work has started at Bicester. An 'exemplar' development of around 300 homes has been built by housing association A2Dominion and Crest Nicholson.

Ebbsfleet

Ebbsfleet in North Kent is one of the worst examples of delay. The 666-acre Eastern Quarry site adjacent the Bluewater shopping centre was bought by Land Securities at the turn of the millennium. Britain's biggest property company had hired the man who developed the nearby Bluewater mega-mall for Lend Lease, Peter Walichnowski. He influenced the purchase of the old cement plant workings next door to the shopping centre. After he left in 2001, Landsec seemed to lose interest, after writing off £96 million filling the giant hole. A total of £275 million of government money is earmarked to be spent between 2016 and 2021. This is on top of the £100 million it cost to build the HS2 station which opened in 2007.

Attempts to get Landsec to commit more fully failed, even after the government set up the Ebbsfleet Development Corporation in 2015. In 2018, Landsec lost interest, selling the remaining 650-odd acres for £68 million to a land trader. The new corporation's vision: 15,000 new homes and '30,000 people working in a green, modern environment around the International Station.' A government review in 2018 gave the development corporation five more years to get up to speed. 'Ebbsfleet seems to be so stultified in its pace of development,' says John Healey, who teased the government in 2018. 'We did a calculation for the number of new homes that have been built since 2010 at Ebbsfleet and the number of announcements that had been made relating to Ebbsfleet. And they were issuing at least one press statement for every seventeen homes they managed to build.'

At the end of 2019 just under 2,000 homes had been built. Of the offices to hold 30,000 workers, there is little sign. A planner who has visited the site said: 'It is pretty depressing; there is plenty of land, God knows, yet all the homes are jammed together on little estates that look like a giant lasso has been dropped around the boundaries and then tightened and tightened.' The answer is, of course, that all the land value has been sucked out by the developers and the builders have been forced to build small and tight.

Letwin proposals

In September 2018, the Letwin review gave birth to a report suggesting that landowners should get no more than ten times the existing use value for their land if permission for homes was granted. An issue discussed in Chapter Five. Sir Oliver also elaborated on the 2017 Housing

White Paper's call for local development corporations, suggesting Local Development Companies (LDCs) supervise garden communities by establishing a masterplan and design code for the site, then bring in private capital to pay for the land and to invest in the infrastructure, then parcel up the site and sell to selected builders/providers – pretty much the 'stewardship' model suggested by Knight Frank at the end of Chapter Two. Alternatively, he suggested, councils could appoint a private company as master-planner, then enable a privately financed Infrastructure Development Company (IDC) to purchase the land from the local authority. In either case, the LDC or IDC sets out the number, size and density of the homes beforehand, thus fixing the price of the land.

Toby Lloyd worked in No 10 as a housing policy advisor during Theresa May's tenure as Prime Minister. Does he feel garden communities could set higher standards by insisting upon homes being built 25% larger than national space standards and densities closer to twenty than thirty to the hectare? 'That is precisely how I would change the world, by not trying to change every single development from the centre, but by leading with some critical exemplar developments that the government has a big hand in.

'The garden communities programme would be an obvious place to start. I disagree that maximum densities are the right rule, but that's a technical point. It is absolutely within the government's power to say, this is how we change the world. Where the government is investing huge amounts of public money, especially for infrastructure, we should be building, not just the average well, but the best. The absolute best.'

Lloyd would like Homes England to take a lead. 'I would use Homes England to strategically acquire all of the land on one or two garden communities, take the legal fight. Show to the market that you mean business and that you don't care how long it will take, and how much in lawyer's fees it will cost. And once you've won that, even if you lose it, but very expensively, you will have sent a very clear signal to the market that this is how it will be. The whole point would be to build more affordable homes, much more environmentally sustainable homes, homes with decent space standards in properly planned and properly maintained places, all of which requires a long-term investment in the stewardship as a whole, really.'

In October 2019, Housing and Communities Secretary Robert Jenrick threw a sprat to Letwin's mackerel, announcing plans to give £10 million in total to the ten local authorities who could come up with the best plans for local development corporations, with money paid to consultants to refine plans. He announced the first at Toton, near East Midlands Airport, chaired by former chairman of Burberry Sir John Peace and aided by Sir George Iacobescu, chairman of Canary Wharf. 'We are looking for up to ten transformational housing and economic growth opportunities,' said Jenrick. Sir Oliver Letwin resigned the Conservative whip in November 2019 and left Parliament during the December 2019 election. A Remainer casualty of the Brexit wars.

Public and Private sector pathways

By far the biggest 'garden communities' push is being led by the public sector in Essex. Three settlements containing a total of 43,000 homes are planned. The effort is being led by Essex County Council and Braintree, Colchester and Tendring District Councils. The three sites are west of Braintree, on the Braintree-Colchester border and on the Colchester-Tendring border. A North Essex Garden Communities (NEGC) board was set up in 2017. Work on-site was scheduled to start in 2021. Alas, in May 2020, a planning inspector dubbed the plans 'unsound' and told the authorities to think again.

A private sector-led solution is being promoted by planners ICENI. The construct is called the Alternative Delivery Model (ADM), an idea that has yet to find a home, so to speak. But at the core of the ADM would sit a controlling Limited Liability Partnership. The LLP is set up with shares divided between the local authority, the land promoter, the landowner and institutional investors. The allocation of shares is structured to allow the parties to reduce and increase their shareholdings, and even exit the company if they can find a buyer. The key to the process is that the increase in the land value can be dealt with at the time the shares are allocated. What gets argued about is the equity split in the LLP, not how many angels you can get on a square inch of land.

Biggleswade

Attentive readers will have spotted on page 106 that co-author Jackie Sadek's development at Biggleswade is on the garden communities list. How did that happen? Jackie Sadek: 'We were beginning to proselytise about the need for children (and everyone, in fact) to be able to run around the country in the fresh air. We avidly read Dieter Helm's *Natural Capital* and had signed up to the programme. We had already pledged to reintroduce more biodiversity than we had inherited. Our vision was for four villages to emerge from a country park and we were only going to be able to develop 40% of the entire site in any case.

'So, one of the things that became clear to us during our discussions was that the landscaping – and the advance planting – were, if anything, more important than the architecture. I went to see Lord Heseltine in his office and asked him to devise me a tree-planting strategy. He joked that he "wasn't in the business of helping property developers" before urging me to keep it simple. His advice could be summarised in one word: oaks! It was most heartening. So, we had been thinking about this for several years.

'And when the government announced a bidding round for places to become "garden communities", we thought Biggleswade was a slam dunk, to be honest, and luckily so did our local authority, as they had to write the submission. We were thrilled to be accorded garden community status by the department in June 2019. Not because it entails a lot of grant money, although there is a welcome £150,000 which will go into the Central Beds Council, but more because it encouraged us in our thinking. And it confers a badge which communicates certain values. It is a badge we wear with pride.'

Prince of Wales cul-de-sac

This chapter began with the Prince of Wales. Let's end with an unpublished tale of his interest in more than just Poundbury. Ian Henderson is a kindly man. In early 2009, the former chief executive of Land Securities asked me if I'd like to chair a 'steering group' set up by a regeneration charity run by the Prince of Wales. I had just vacated the editor's chair at *Estates Gazette* after eleven years. The first meeting was held in a chilly garret under the eaves at St James's Palace. About fifteen folks had squeezed into the tiny room. Some were housebuilders, some planners, others worked for pension funds. HRH's instructions were to come up with a model that could be used to build large-scale settlements – like Poundbury.

A few meetings followed, held in the offices of Knight Frank in Baker Street. Head of Research Liam Bailey had agreed that Knight Frank would publish a report. The tentative findings? Housebuilders are not interested in acting as lead developer on large-scale settlements. 'Enabling companies' are needed to lead joint ventures, which include partners with money, planning skills, development skills and, of course, a partner who owns the land. There was a consensus that capturing the uplift on land values was vital if you wanted to build at Poundbury quality. Then it all went quiet. Nothing was published. Not that it mattered; these ideas were already in the air.

SEVEN

PRIVATE HOMES

'Capitalism has forced everyone to overoptimize in order to compete.'
Nassim Nicholas Taleb, author of *The Black Swan*

Why blame private developers for not building enough homes? Developers are in business to make a profit. They do this by balancing risk and reward, which means having enough land in the planning bank for the foreseeable future. Then, by not building more than they can sell at an economic rate, a rate determined by the highest price achievable at the time. Don't wholly blame developers for building small, squeezed-together homes. Without state-imposed minimum sizes and density ceilings, housebuilders tend to squeeze in order to compete for land, mechanisms explained in Chapters One and Two.

Reaching the magic number

A target of 300,000 new homes a year by 'the mid-2020s' shimmers on the government's horizon. Can it be reached? Assume compound growth rates of 9% for the private sector, from 2019, 10% for housing association and 20% for council building – the answer (overleaf) comes out at 306,000. Housebuilders need to reach 243,000 by 2025 from 145,000 in 2019. Councils require a modest uplift from 3,000 to 7,000. Housing associations need to jump from 33,000 to 50,000. Given the 'Grenfell' challenges they face (Chapter Nine), that feels unlikely.

Estimate of completions by 2025

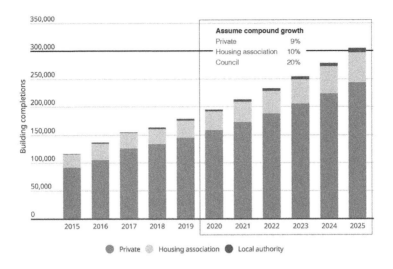

Source: ONS plus estimates

Forget the target if chill economic winds blow. Ignore the deep dig at the start of the storm of the coronavirus pandemic. Between 2006 and 2009, starts fell from 205,000 to 89,000, and prices dropped by up to 45% in that economic crash. Collateral damage was then inflicted on the 'affordable' sector. Developers can't afford to build affordable homes if the private units are not selling. Neither can they afford to pay Section 106 or the Community Infrastructure Levy.

Bash the builder

Housebuilders are seen as fair game to be shot at by politicians for not building enough homes. Now and again they are called in front of MPs to explain themselves. A light grilling by the House of Commons Communities and Local Government Select Committee informed the 'Capacity in the homebuilding industry' report published in the spring of 2017. Were housebuilders the devils' spawn, or not? Hard to tell from the ambivalent findings.

On the one hand: 'The eight largest firms build more than half of all new homes, which means we are overly reliant on an alarmingly small number of commercial actors.' On the other hand: 'There is little incentive for housebuilders to build any quicker. It is in their commercial self-interest to maintain profits and they cannot be blamed for this.'

On the one hand: 'The high-volume homebuilders dominate the market and are therefore able to shape how it operates.' On the other hand: 'This is rational commercial behaviour and a sound business model.' However, this is not in the country's best interests. These would be best served by reducing 'the dominance of the high-volume builders by encouraging a far greater mix of developers'.

Former Conservative MP Mark Prisk sat on the select committee. He explains: 'We were doing social care at the time. I have a feeling this became slightly number two in people's priorities and it was therefore left to the clerks to write something that was sort of balanced.'

Taylor Wimpey and Barratt

Taylor Wimpey's Pete Redfern told MP's, 'Look if you want to put capital to work in our sector, it takes a long time and the levels of uncertainty are too high. We cannot throw money at things when we have a high degree of uncertainty.' Barratt boss David Thomas gently teased the committee: 'If the government provides a proposition that is substantially lower risk, then developers will build houses at lower margins. Currently, we are effectively speculative builders. We are taking all the sales risk: can we or can't we sell the houses?'

In October 2017, the government responded by agreeing to once again reform the planning system and also to ask planning authorities to 'monitor' build-out rates. Pointless, concedes Mark Prisk. 'If the truth be told, ministers can't pull that lever. But they want to be seen to be doing something – and that's why they always have a go at planning reform. It's almost obligatory to do that. I think it would be better if we could get away from the notion of we're going to fix something. But, that's political rhetoric for you.'

Barratt had prepared a defence against the committee's main charge of land hoarding and speculation. 'The role of land pipelines in the UK housebuilding process' is enlightening. In early 2017, only 286,000 of the 546,000 plots with detailed permission were owned by housebuilders. The other 260,000 were in the hands of those wishing to sell them to housebuilders. Only 13% of the 130,000 plots with outline permission were held by housebuilders.

Land banking

'Why do builders need to hold 60,000 plots of land if they are only building 15,000 a year?' is the cry of those who accuse housebuilders of hoarding land. Because it takes at least four years from land purchase to home sales, says Barratt. If you are expanding at just 5% a year, the land bank needed stretches from four years to 4.5 years. The land pipeline document lays out the four distinct stages in the process:

A: Finding a site to lodging an application – fifteen to twenty-five months.
B: Getting permission – six to nine months.
C: From consent to construction – six to twenty-one months.
D: Start work to finishing typical site – twelve to twenty-seven months.

Sites that whoosh through the pipeline can make it in three years and three months. Sluggish sites can take six years and nine months. Stage C is little understood. Pre-commencement conditions are often attached to the permission in the Section 106 Agreement. 'Before you start a single house we want you to build our stuff – here is a list.' Also, 'conditions' need to be met, meaning, 'permission granted – but need to have another look at X and Y before you start'.

Length of time between land purchase and home sales

Model part 1: length of the development pipeline

A simple development pipeline - with four distinct phases - can be depicted as in Figure 1, below:

Figure 1: Illustrative development pipeline

Development stages	Time periods								
	1	2	3	4	5	6	7	8	9
Pre-application									
Application to permission									
From permission to start on site									
Under construction									
Completion of new home(s)									

If it is assumed that each phase lasts one period (e.g. a year) Figure 1 shows that in year five the builder has its first completion (from scheme 1).

But in order to maintain production at a constant rate beyond year five, Figure 2 shows that the builder must have four newer schemes underway, each in a different phase:

Figure 2: Land bank associated with illustrative development pipeline

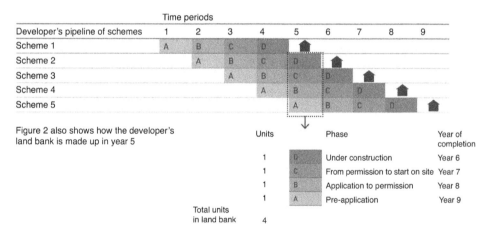

Figure 2 also shows how the developer's land bank is made up in year 5

	Units	Phase	Year of completion
	1	D: Under construction	Year 6
	1	C: From permission to start on site	Year 7
	1	B: Application to permission	Year 8
	1	A: Pre-application	Year 9
Total units in land bank	4		

Source: Barratt Developments

Philip Barnes is responsible for keeping the 80,000-plot land bank topped up at Britain's largest housebuilder. 'Land is the largest investment for development and therefore as soon as the cheque is cashed the pressure is on the business to move quickly to build and sell, in order to return the capital deployed,' says Barratt's group land and planning director.

'Sitting on land simply increases those costs with no guarantee of higher revenues at the other end. Where delays do occur, they are due either to the planning process or unforeseen ground problems rather than any desire to land bank.'

The pace of sales is controlled by the number of sales per outlet per week, or SPOW. These sales rates have not changed in decades. If sales rise, prices are notched up to slow SPOW. If the market slows, prices are kept static and discounts such as 'finishing touches' vouchers to buy furniture, or upgrade the kitchen, or the more naked 'deposit contribution' is offered, all done to maintain the budgeted SPOW.

Land banks, land supply, outlets, sales per outlet per week (SPOW)

	2017/18	2018/19	2017/18	2018/19	2017/18	2018/19	2018/19
	Plots		Land supply, years		Outlets		SPOW
Barratt	79,432	80,022	4.8	4.7	380	379	0.7
Persimmon	98,445	99,098	6.1	6	375	360	0.75
Taylor Wimpey	74,849	76,000	5.4	5.1	288	256	0.8
Bellway	41,077	42,721	2.4	2.4	247	268	1.2
Redrow	27,630	31,500	4.8	4.9	124	129	0.96
Countryside	19,778	24,304	4.6	4.2	53	56	0.84
Totals	341,211	353,645			1,467	1,448	

Source: company accounts

Philip Barnes explains the central role sales rates play. 'A site sale rate is determined when we bid for a site, part of the initial budget, when build cost and revenue assumptions are made. After purchase, the aim is to achieve the budget build costs and sales rates, with the resources available. Strength of demand, the build team and supply chain capacity, weather, and levels of competition can all affect the sales rate.

'So, whilst the idea of fast sales rates capitalising on strong demand sounds attractive, it can also create problems down the line by creating pressure on the build teams and risking quality for the customer. These are risks we won't take. So, we concentrate on achieving budget targets rather than the fastest possible pace of build. Put simply, our focus is always on the customer rather than simply maximising how many homes can be sold.'

Near-death experience

Housebuilders have not forgotten the crash of 2007/08. Barratt shares were worth 1,260p in January 2007; by July 2008, they had crashed to 16p. Taylor Wimpey shares were 518p in April 2007 and 9p in December 2008. Both came close to corporate death. The Great Crash, which began in the summer of 2007 and petered out in 2012, remains seared into the corporate memory of major housebuilders. Taylor Wimpey posted a loss of £1.8 billion in 2008 – followed by another £503 million loss in 2009. Barratt declared a loss of £485 million in June 2009. Both were kept from drowning in debt only by banks who had enough trouble of their own.

When the coronavirus pandemic hit in March 2020, ten years of caution and seven years of plenty had at least left them is a far stronger financial position. In the Spring of 2020, Barratt had £380 million in the bank, Persimmon £610 million and Taylor Wimpey £165 million. The trio also had agreed on overdrafts to draw from, totalling well over £2 billion. During March and April reservations dropped to around one-third of normal levels. But, all three reported strong forward sales and began opening sites in early May.

Near-nemesis in the 2007/9 crash had been preceded by hubris. In the spring of 2007, Wimpey and Taylor Woodrow merged. The new, £5 billion business boasted 14,000 staff, then employed in building 22,000 homes a year. A substantial part of Taylor Woodrow's operations was in the US. New home sales in America were falling, and the word 'sub-prime' was already in the air. But no matter: the 'underlying' market was reportedly stable in both the UK and the US.

Taylor Wimpey boss Pete Redfern, then thirty-six and still running the business in early 2020, got to run the combined company. Only 700 job losses were expected as a result of the merger. The shares stood at over 500p. Then: crash, bang! The US business was sold. Staff numbers were cut to 3,500. The shares hit a low of 9p by December 2008. Redfern then pledged a profit-first, volume-second policy.

Barratt paid £2.2 billion to acquire Leicester-based housebuilder Wilson Bowden in February 2007. The purchase was masterminded by Mark Clare, an approachable accountant who had joined Barratt from British Gas in the summer of 2006. Wilson Bowden co-founder David Wilson and his family were fortunate enough to take £198 million in cash as part of the deal – but unfortunate enough to take £271 million in Barratt shares too, then valued at over £12.50 each. Within six months, the market and share price was tumbling. By July 2008, the shares had plunged to 16p. When Barratt got itself back into the black again in 2010, Clare also pledged to do things differently: profit first, scale second.

Golden years

The seven financial years between 2012/13 and 2018/19 proved golden years. Barratt, Bellway, Berkeley, Countryside, Crest, Galliford, Miller and Persimmon made a combined profit of £15.6 billion, earned by selling 291,000 homes at an average margin of £53,500 per unit. By 2018, the top ten were all making profits of over 20% – and being attacked in the press for doing so, because the reputations of some were as low as the profits of all were high.

Gross margin as a percentage of the sales price

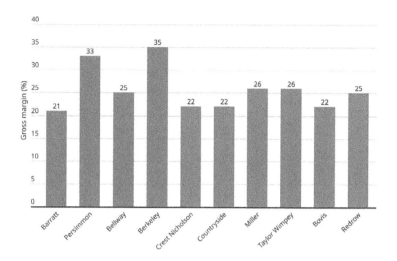

Costs as a percentage of the sales price

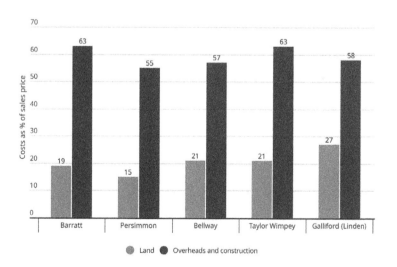

Source: company accounts

State Help to Build

Former Labour Shadow Housing Secretary John Healey declines to attack housebuilders profits, but, 'I think you can criticise them and require more of them, on the jobs and training they offer, the poor-quality shoddy work they do, as they try and cut corners. Their reluctance to recognise that they operate as businesses within a modern society in which there are certain obligations, as well as the responsibilities that they've got to their shareholders. An industry that prides itself on being a capitalist market is also hugely dependent on government subsidies to help survive.'

John Healey has a point. By the summer of 2019, £759 million had been allocated from a £2.3 billion Homes England Housing Infrastructure Fund for 'Marginal Viability Funding', money being spent on 110 projects to 'unlock' a suspiciously accurate figure of 119,134 homes. In plain English: the taxpayer is paying for roads and utilities that cannot be afforded within the 'viability' model, which allows a developer to make 20% profit on the private homes and 6–7% on the affordable units.

That said, the state effectively gives with one hand and takes away with the other. At its most simplistic, the residual land value is pumped up by the taxpayer funding new roads to make the land 'viable'. Then the land value is deflated by the amount the state takes to build new schools and affordable homes. One of the ways to illustrate the way this works is to examine the illustration produced by Shelter in a 2017 report, 'New Civic Housebuilding', produced by then-Director of Policy, Toby Lloyd – a report that directly led to Lloyd being offered a job in No 10. Shelter's agenda was not to make you feel sorry for the landowner. But, as the illustration shows, the residual land value halves if the number of affordable homes on a 500-unit site goes up from 15% to 50%. Section 106 payments have the same effect.

Impact on land values of varying affordable home numbers

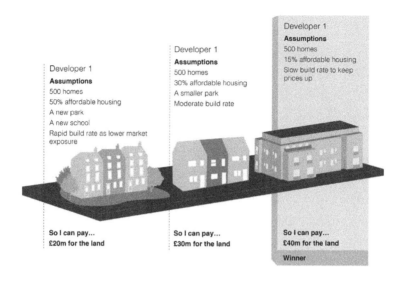

Developer 1

Assumptions

500 homes

50% affordable housing

A new park

A new school

Rapid build rate as lower market exposure

So I can pay...

£20m for the land

Developer 1

Assumptions

500 homes

30% affordable housing

A smaller park

Moderate build rate

So I can pay...

£30m for the land

Developer 1

Assumptions

500 homes

15% affordable housing

Slow build rate to keep prices up

So I can pay...

£40m for the land

Winner

Source: Shelter: 'New Civic Housebuilding'

State Help to Buy

Giving equity-backed loans to first-time buyers has long been a vote winner. In 2013, the government introduced the Help to Buy variant administered by Homes England. First-time buyers are advanced up to 20% of the price up to a limit of £600,000. In London, the loan can be up to 40% of the price. The buyer pays 1.75% interest on the twenty-five-year loan. If your home doubles in price, the capital amount of the loan you pay back also doubles. If the price falls, the amount needed to be repaid falls in parallel. Lower price caps have been introduced from April 2021 on Help to Buy, which is scheduled to end in April 2023.

By March 2020, equity loans of £16.05 billion had been advanced against 272,852 properties worth £73 billion. Fortunes may await the taxpayer when the state's stakes are sold. Or not. In February 2020, the scheme was rebadged 'First Homes' by Housing Secretary Robert Jenrick. First-time buyers will be offered a 30% discount on the open-market price of the house. This more restricted scheme is due to be introduced in 2021. Buyers will have to be 'local', whatever that is meant to mean, or be armed forces veterans or key workers, such as nurses, police officers and firefighters. The discount will be locked into the house price in perpetuity via an attachment to the deeds.

Help to profit

Housing analyst Alastair Stewart found the gross margins of the biggest housebuilders had jumped from the 13–19% range in 2013 to the 20–30% range by 2019. Stewart calculated Help to Buy allowed builders to charge 3–5% more. An abstruse academic paper 'showed Help to Buy increased prices by 3.2–3.9% proved by the formulae Ln (Price) I = Treati + f (Distance) + ui', according to the Bartlett School of Construction. There is an easier way. The top six have put up prices by 53% since 2012 – 4% ahead of the general market increase of 49%.

Price growth March 2013–19: top six housebuilders vs the price growth of all housing

AVERAGE PRICE -000	13	14	15	16	17	18	19	Seven-year uplift
Barratt	197	220	235	260	275	288	274	39%
Persimmon	176	182	191	199	207	213	215	22%
Taylor Wimpey	181	194	214	230	257	267	264	46%
Bellway	193	213	224	253	260	291	284	47%
Redrow	212	240	270	289	310	332	324	53%
Countryside	178	213	232	253	250	402	367	107%
SIX AVERAGE	189	210	228	247	260	299	288	**53%**
ALL AVERAGE	168	178	191	206	227	244	251	**49%**

Source: company reports and house price data

Increasing numbers

The government has complained that the number of firms building private homes has dropped from over 6,000 to 2,000 since 1996. Back in 1996, market supply was evenly balanced: big builders 35%, medium-sized builders 40% and small builders 25%. By 2019, the volume builders' market share was over 60% and small builders sold less than 10%. Why worry? The number of completions rose strongly between 2013 and 2019. Not just among the top six. The 'others' pretty much kept up.

Completions: England, March 2013–19

COMPLETIONS	13	14	15	16	17	18	19
Barratt	13,663	14,838	16,047	17,319	17,395	17,856	17,579
Persimmon	9,903	11,528	13,509	14,572	15,171	16,043	16,449
Taylor Wimpey	10,886	11,665	12,458	13,470	14,112	14,688	15,275
Bellway	5,652	6,851	7,752	8,721	9,644	10,307	10,892
Redrow	2,827	3,597	4,022	4,716	5,416	5,718	6,443
Countryside	1,560	2,034	2,364	2,657	3,389	4,295	5,733
TOP SIX	44,491	50,513	56,152	61,455	65,127	68,907	72,371
OTHERS	64,194	69,526	84,333	80,230	82,120	92,273	101,289
TOTAL	108,685	120,039	140,485	141,685	147,247	161,180	173,660

Source: company accounts and ONS data

'Capitalism at its worst'

Persimmon boss Jeff Fairburn was famously forced out in 2018 not long after taking £75 million in pay and share bonuses. A lack of repentance cost him his job after complaints about the quality of Persimmon Homes became widespread. The board hired Stephanie Barwise QC to conduct a review. A government threat to drop them from the lucrative Help to Buy scheme may have helped. In December 2019, the barrister reported that Persimmon had been 'more a seller of houses than a housebuilder', and a 'culture of non-observance and box-ticking was a manifestation of poor culture'.

The *FT* called for the head of the man who took over from Fairburn, David Jenkinson. In a leader headed 'Persimmon report shows capitalism at its worst', the FT suggested, 'The board should consider if David Jenkinson, the current CEO who has been at Persimmon for more than two decades, is the right man to drive the change required.' In early 2020, Jenkinson announced he was going to retire after twenty-three years. The FT also took the Home Builders Federation (HBF) to task, suggesting the organisation 'reviews the way it awards stars based on buyers' satisfaction. The idea that a trade lobby group is going to flagellate one of its biggest members is naïve. The HBF is there to look after the interests of its members, not its members' customers.'

The Home Builders Federation tends to circle the wagons when attacked, on the not-unreasonable assumption that their approval ratings are as low as those of journalists and estate agents. But those in the trade know there are significant cultural and behavioural differences among the housebuilders. Some CEOs chase growth; others chase profit. Some concentrate on cost-cutting; others focus on quality. Some like to hold all the reins; others are content with federated regions. Some stick to doing right by themselves; some like to do right by customers and suppliers.

In the 1980s, Barratt's reputation was that of Persimmon today. Back in the 1980s, Persimmon had a fine reputation, built by its founder Duncan Davidson, the bespectacled fifteenth grandson of the Duke of Norfolk. Today it's Barratt's chief executive David Thomas who can say without blushing, 'We aim to lead the future of housebuilding by putting the customer at the heart of everything; whether that's through embracing new technologies, designing communities or giving nature a home. We want to lead the housebuilding industry.'

Modern methods of construction

By early 2020, momentum was building on what is called Modern Methods of Construction, or MMC for short. By then, the late Tony Pidgley had a factory in north Kent to supply the various arms of the Berkeley Group with kits of parts. Many others had been investing in ways of transferring work from mucky sites to clean factories. Insurance giant Legal & General had led the way in 2015. Boss Nigel Wilson was an enthusiast, keen to power up L&G's Build to Rent portfolio. He set up L&G Modular Homes. By the turn of the decade, Wilson's enthusiasm had cost L&G £90 million in write-downs. The 500,000 square foot factory near Leeds was supposed to be turning out 3,000 homes a year by 2020 but wasn't.

By 2020, the leading insurer of new homes, NHBC, had registered forty-four different MMC methods. Each had to pass a series of tests before getting the NHBC's stamp of approval. With this stamp, mortgage companies would more readily grant loans. What worries many is that it will take only a single scandal to bring the entire sector into disrepute despite these safeguards. For these reasons, the biggest housebuilders were still steering more slowly. Barratt is typical. In February 2020, they pledged to use MMC to build 25% of their homes by 2025. In the second half of 2019, Barratt was building 17.6% of homes with MMC methods, mostly by the use of timber frame.

Gearing up output

Suppliers of homes to housing associations and councils are moving faster. In early 2020, the NHBC arranged a presentation on MMC by Dave Sheridan of ilke Homes, a mid-sized Yorkshire builder which has built an MMC factory near Halifax, with the aid of a £30 million government grant. The factory operates a two-shift system, from six in the morning until ten at night. They are 'geared up' to build 1,000 units a year but were not doing so at the time.

Sheridan said the business becomes 'cash neutral' at 1,000 units a year, using 600 workers. When output reaches 2,000 units a year, the workforce only needs to rise to 850, he said. Those buying his MMC homes will end up with on-site construction costs from £650 per square metre in the north, to £1,000 per square metre in London. Much the same as traditional construction asserted Sheridan. But, 'MMC homes can be built at twice the speed of traditionally built units, meaning landlords can start collecting rent earlier. These homes are 23% more energy-efficient, saving tenants a fortune in heating costs.'

Farmer report

The leading proponent of MMC is Mark Farmer, a former partner at cost consultants E.C. Harris, now running his cost consultancy, Cast. Farmer produced a seventy-five-page report on MMC for government in October 2016 called 'Modernise or Die'. The 'ticking time bomb' facing the construction industry was the 20–25% reduction in the workforce during the 2020s, he warned. Baby-boomer bricklayers and carpenters who were apprenticed in the 1960s and 1970s are retiring. Over 30% of the workforce is over fifty. The tide of immigrant labour is receding. The flow of youngsters into the trade is too little to prevent the time bomb going off. The only answer, concluded Farmer, was to build factory-assembled homes.

Your authors visited Mark Farmer in late October 2019 at his offices close to London's diamond district, Hatton Garden. We came away impressed by his articulacy, enthusiasm and grasp. MMC is the coming thing, despite the reluctance of more conservative housebuilders. Mark looked dressed for a wedding. We asked why? He was off to see Housing Minister Esther McVey. A couple of days later, McVey announced plans for a 'hub' in the north of England to promote MMC. Farmer was at the event held at Sheffield University. He said, 'The UK has a fantastic opportunity to become a true world leader in the advanced manufacturing of new homes.' A few days later Farmer was appointed 'government champion' to promote MMC. A few weeks later, Esther McVey was sacked.

Her replacement, Christopher Pincher, is equally enthusiastic. The MP for Tamworth commissioned Homes England in May 2020 to carry out long term research into MMC. Seven sites using various methods of prefabrication will be monitored. 'Modern methods of construction have enormous potential to not only accelerate this work but to deliver better quality homes too,' said Pincher. 'Such an extensive and practical study will no doubt inform housebuilding for years to come.'

Ground rents

Ground rents have been around since Roman Times. In the commercial property sector, there has been a steady trade in the rights to charge rents for hundreds of years. The 1967 and 2002 Leasehold Reform Acts now govern how they are charged. These rights tend to change hands, typically at auction, at around twenty to twenty-five times the annual charge, bringing a 'yield' to the buyer of 4–5%. Ground rents have also been around forever on new homes in certain parts of the country. I used to pay a fixed £32 a year for my Wimpey home in Bristol in the 1970s.

The trouble began about fifteen years ago when some housebuilders began to insert clauses in their sales agreements allowing the ground rent holder to effectively double the charge every ten years, so hugely jacking up the value to an investor. Selling a ground rent yielding £200 a year might raise £4,000. Selling one with a prospective yield of £2,000 a year might raise a great deal more. Stories began to appear of owners not being able to sell their homes because the buyer's solicitor figured the ground rent might hit £10,000 a year in thirty or forty years.

Around 2012, those in the quiet backwater of commercial ground rent trading began to be disturbed by the actions of housebuilders. 'Bloody idiots, spoiling it for us all,' was the cry. Stories of leaseholder rage reverberated through the media, encouraged by the Leasehold Knowledge Partnership, an effective lobby group run by former *Mail on Sunday* property editor Sebastian O'Kelly. Such was the furore generated, the government effectively banned housebuilders from selling homes with ground rents in 2019.

Back in 2017, Taylor Wimpey was forced to set up a £130 million compensation scheme, promising recompense and apologising for 'the unintended financial consequence and concern they are causing'. In 2019, the Competition and Markets Authority (CMA) opened an investigation, demanding evidence from those who sold leasehold instead of freehold. Later in the year the CMA opened 'enforcement cases' against Barratt, Countryside, Persimmon and Taylor Wimpey. The CMA's concerns included:

- 'Ground rents which significantly rise over time. The consequences of such obligations can be severe for homeowners, creating difficulty in selling or mortgaging their homes.

- 'Numerous complaints about developers mis-selling leasehold houses. Many matters complained of are said to have influenced the behaviour of purchasers early in the sales process.

Proposals by the Law Commission to radically reform the law were published in July 2020. The central proposal in the 800-page report was to allow leaseholders to extend their lease from 90 to 990 years - with no ground rent attached. The government promised to enact 'when Parliamentary time allowed.'

Build to Rent

Back in 2006, Chancellor Gordon Brown tried to stimulate a debate on the rental sector. One way of airing the arguments was by using the Smith Institute think tank run by his friend and advisor, Wilf Stevenson. At a No 11 breakfast on 17th May 2006, Housing Minister Yvette Cooper and senior civil servants gathered there to listen attentively to the experts who had contributed to 'More Homes for Rent', a Smith Institute publication I'd edited.

The central recommendation was a separate planning use class for rented homes – a proposal put forward by Alan Collett of agent Allsop and William Hill of Schroders bank. This planning restriction would depress the land value for rented homes to below that of the open market price, allowing Build to Rent (BTR) developers to buy land at prices which made it economic to build rented homes. Civil servants squashed that idea. Undaunted, the Smith Institute had another go. The 'Future of the Private Rented Sector', in 2008, included the same recommendation from Mark Long of fund manager Invista, who suggested a form of licensing scheme. One which would oblige developers to rent the homes for a fixed number of years. *Nada.*

In 2010, the Conservative-led coalition tried once more. Incoming Housing Minister Grant Shapps turned out to be an unusually accessible minister. An email arrived one Saturday morning in June 2010 from the man himself. He wanted contact details for Jackie Sadek, *Broken Homes* co-author. I pinged him back, adding something along the lines of, 'I know your job is a bugger and your diary a nightmare. But if you want to have a relaxing and highly amusing lunch, invite Jackie.' Ping! 'I will – and will you come as well?'

Lunch with Housing Minister

In October, Jackie and I had lunch with Shapps at Portcullis House. I was not privy to what happened next. But in early 2011, an article in *EG* revealed Shapps was endorsing a £3 billion plan to build 20,000 BTR homes constructed by Sadek's company, UK Regeneration. You can read all about what did and what didn't happen in Chapter Eight. Shapps was replaced in July 2012 by Mark Prisk. 'One of the first questions I asked,' said Prisk, 'was do we now need to make it a wholly separate asset class? And my instinct was, well, hang on a moment. We've only just created this thing and if we start creating barriers to exit before we've got enough people investing, you're going to put people off. We've got to get people in and feel comfortable that they can exit their investment.

'I used to work with Reg Ward, who was the chief executive of the LDDC. What Reg said was that when he was trying to get people to invest in Docklands, he said, "You have to remember, the institutions are a bit like sheep. Once you've got the first sheep in the pen with a bell around his neck, the others will come. But getting that first one in is bloody difficult." He was right. I was worried about closing off the pen by making it a separate asset class.'

In 2012, a very big sheep plodded into the pen. Qatar's state developer, Qatari Diar, and Jamie Ritblat's Delancey bought over 1,400 new homes in the athletes' village on the Olympic Park, saying they would rent them out after the games. Funds began to prick up their ears. By April 2020, the pen was filling nicely. Over 157,000 Build to Rent homes were in the pipeline, including the 43,000 completed in 2019 – up from 30,000 the year before.

In 1999, Savills predicted the number of UK renters would increase by a million to reach 3.2 million by 2012. At the turn of the century, funds were seeking returns in the 8–11% range. Two decades of low-interest rates had now persuaded them 5–6% is fine – a yield which allows BTR investors to compete for land with build to sell buyers. Turned out a new use class was not needed. Funds like Legal & General, M&G and US supplier Greystar have moved heavily into build to rent.

Grainger example

A ride on the Jubilee Line from Canning Town to Green Park Station takes twenty-one minutes. You could rise from your sofa in your Argo apartment in the East End of London and emerge blinking on Piccadilly half an hour later. In the summer of 2019, I travelled in the reverse direction to meet Helen Gordon, chief executive of Grainger, at their fifteen-storey Argo block containing 134 rented flats, completed earlier in the year. Gordon has transformed the UK's largest residential landlord since joining in 2016. By 2020, Grainger has a BTR pipeline of 9,000 units. In 2019, over 1,100 were built. We spend an hour walking the floors. The Argo flats cost £33 million to build – about £250,000 apiece. They were 97% let within four months. The gross yield is 8%. Costs are budgeted to clip no more than 26% off the gross, taking the net yield down to just under 6%. The rents range from £1,450 a month for a one-bed to £1,800 for a two-bed. 'We base the rents on the average pay levels in the area,' says Gordon. 'The minimum household salary for a one-bed is £43,000 and for a two-bed £51,000.'

Permitted development rights

What a good idea, I thought back in 2014: let developers throw off town-hall shackles and convert empty office blocks into homes without the need to consult bothersome planners. Fill in a form telling the council you are going to start work. Pop in the post with a very small cheque, and off you go. What could go wrong? I was not the only person to think about the expansion of Permitted Development Rights as a Good Thing. Pound signs began to appear before the eyes of real estate investors. An empty 50,000 square foot office block you might one day be able to let for £10 square foot per year was worth no more than £7 million. Spend £3 million on a quick conversion and, at £300 square feet for outright sale the residential value of the block would be £15 million. Investors began to buy up likely blocks ahead of legislation enacted in May 2013, then as a temporary three-year measure.

A bonfire of planning regulations had already been made: 1,300 pages of bumf reduced to a fifty-page set of National Planning Policy Framework in 2012 by Planning Minister Greg Clark. Nick Boles, then a Parliamentary Private Secretary, got to roll out PDR. On 13th May 2014, I'd had a meeting on the terrace of the House of Commons with Greg Clark, by then Cities Minister. An admiration for both men, which remains, coloured this comment in my *Estates Gazette* column:

'When Greg Clark was Planning Minister, he was rightly applauded for cutting red tape. His successor, Nick Boles, is likely

to be praised for introducing permitted development rights. PDR applications have exploded since the three-year experiment was introduced by Boles last June. Knight Frank has now gathered data from forty-one local authorities, showing PDR applications totalling 3.1 million square feet have been lodged. Experts say much of the activity is just developers establishing a change of use before going for planning permission. Even so, the numbers are huge.'

May 2014, *Estates Gazette*

In July 2014, Housing Minister Brandon Lewis promised the rules would be made permanent. Developers kept on buying. In 2015, those early in the game began to cash in their chips. Ben Habib became a Brexit Party MEP in 2019. The Cambridge-educated property fund manager told me a PDR fund set up by his First Property Group had bought eight sub-prime office blocks, starting in 2012, for a total of £30 million. They were all sold by 2015 for £56m in total, with designs for 655 units – for others to convert, not Habib.

Inhumanity

Who gave a thought to those who would occupy what then became known as Permitted Development (PD) units? Who would have thought that an absence of controls would see developers building flats of 150 square feet? How could anyone be inhumane enough to house individuals in offices on industrial estates, or next to twelve-lane trunk roads? Not those who drafted the rules. Decent surveyors began to be horrified at what they were being asked to approve for loans. The Royal Institution of Chartered Surveyors set up an inquiry. In May 2018, the RICS spoke out after examining 500 'PD' schemes.

'There were some high-quality developments. However, PD has also allowed extremely poor-quality housing to be developed. The comparison showed that PD residential quality was significantly worse than schemes which required planning permission'. Evidence of this reduction in quality included:

- Studio flats just fifteen metres square or sixteen metres square.
- No access to private or communal amenity space.
- Residential developments on industrial estates.
- 77% of units are studio or one-bedroom flats.

Chartered surveyors tend not to be tree-huggers. But the RICS recommendations conveys their shock: 'The policy of office-to-residential change should be returned to full planning control.' If not, 'Adding minimum space standards which would apply even to PD schemes.'

Julia Park of Levitt Bernstein drew attention to the issue in *Building Design* after visiting a PD scheme in West London:

'Having arrived early for a site visit and design review in Newbury Park, at lunchtime on a blisteringly hot Wednesday, I thought I'd explore the area. Opposite the station, on the edge of the A12, one of the busiest, most polluting roads in London, I noticed a seven-storey office block with curtains drawn across most of the windows. It looked lived-in and above the traffic noise, I could just hear voices inside, including those of children.

'Back in the office, a quick search of Redbridge's planning records confirmed that a request for Prior Approval, to convert the building from office to residential use under Permitted Development (PD), was nodded through by the council in 2014. Each of the six upper floors now comprises ten self-contained, one-roomed studio flats. The architect's drawing describes eighteen of the studios as "singles" and forty-two as "doubles".

'The smallest single is thirteen square metres and the smallest double is 14.7 square metres. Only one is over twenty square metres. All are single aspect with full-width windows. The flats which face north receive no sunlight and the half that face south are exposed to the sun for most of the day. There are no balconies and no shared outdoor space for what is intended to be more than 100 residents; the "site" is just the footprint of the building and the open, ground floor undercroft is full of rubbish.

'I don't know who lives in Newbury House, but it's fair to assume that the majority will have no realistic alternative due to the lack of social housing. An exercise on the government's online calculator reveals that a single adult over thirty-five is entitled to £160.24 per week for housing costs. To get a sense of how lucrative this can be, if Newbury House was fully let to single people in receipt of the one-bedroom rate, the annual rent from the sixty studios would be a few pence short of half a million pounds. I don't know who lives here or what they pay, and that isn't the point. The fact is that no one should have to live like this.'

Julia Park, Building Design, August 2018

Not fit for living

Nick Raynsford is chairman of the Town and Country Planning Association. The former Labour Housing Minister raised another example in early 2020: 'There is this squalid industrial building in Watford, one storey with a roof area covered by what looks like corrugated asbestos. The developer has obtained PDR consent, after appeal. The planning inspectorate was forced to approve fifteen very cramped units, six of which are in this roof space, after the council had refused a licence. The inspector had no grounds to say no. A complete scandal – condemnation of a system, producing squalid substandard homes.

'They won't be occupied by tenants because the tenants would be able to use the fit for human rights legislation to get the properties closed. But that only applies to tenancies. The owners will instead use the place as licensed premises for homeless applicants, who have no say, no choice. That leaves me with a very nasty taste in my mouth.'

The third week in July is the traditional moment governments hang out both clean and dirty washing on the line. On 21st July 2020 the Ministry of Housing published long-trailed plans to expand Permitted Development Rights. Householders would be able to add two floors without applying for formal planning permission. Developers would be able to buy up empty high street shops and convert them into homes using PDR. The same day the ministry published a true horror story on the impact of PDR. Since 2015 more than 60,000 flats have been created through PDR in England, with almost 90% coming from office conversions.

The 213-page report is called 'Research into the quality standards of homes delivered through change of use permitted development.' The authors were Dr Ben Clifford, Dr Patricia Canelas, Dr Jessica Ferm and Dr Nicola Livingstone of the Bartlett School of Planning, along with Professor Alex Lord and Dr Richard Dunning of Liverpool University. Visits were made to 639 PDR conversions.

The results were shocking. Only 22% of these 'homes' satisfied the Nationally Described Space Standards, (NDSS). The remainder were 'significantly below' NDSS levels with studio flats of just sixteen square metres found on a number of schemes. It gets worse. Close to three-quarters of the flats only had a window on one wall. Worse still: 'schemes had layouts that would reduce natural light, for example, contrived layouts to enable the unit to have a window that was far removed from the main useable floor space.' An example given was New Horizons Court in Brentford, where 25 flats have windows facing the central atrium. Under 4% of the schemes had access to private amenity space.

'The new legislation fundamentally undermines the notion of a democratic, professional and accountable planning system,' said Dr Clifford, who co-led the research. 'Not only will it continue to produce more tiny flats with poor living conditions, but it also means the developers are not required to provide any affordable housing or make any contributions to local infrastructure, like parks and play-grounds.'

Suffer little children

In August 2019, Children's Commissioner for England Anne Longfield produced a report, 'Bleak Houses', condemning PD conversions, mentioning, 'Harlow, where more than half of all new homes being created are office block conversions. The council has identified at least thirteen office blocks that have been converted, creating more than 1,000 individual flats. There is a high demand for temporary accommodation in these blocks from central London councils seeking alternatives to higher-cost rents within their boroughs.

'This has led to accusations that areas such as Harlow are being used to "socially cleanse" the capital, with families being required to move far from home. Many of the flats are small, single rooms which do not come close to meeting national space standards. For example, some of the flats in Templefields House measure as little as eighteen square metres – a space which may be shared by a whole family, with parents and children living and sleeping in the same room also containing their cooking facilities and a toilet/shower cubicle.'

EIGHT

JACKIE'S JOURNEY

'How often I found where I should be going only by setting out for somewhere else.'

Architect R. Buckminster Fuller

Jacqueline Elizabeth Sadek. DOB July 1958. Married, three children. Chief operating officer, UK Regeneration. Advisor to UK government 2014–16. Chief executive UK Regeneration 2010–14. Head of Regeneration CBRE 2007–10. Chief executive: Park Royal Partnership 2005–07; Kent Thameside Delivery Board 2004–05; Brierley Hill Regeneration Partnership 2002–04; Paddington Regeneration Partnership 1997–2002. Corporate Affairs Director, Tesco, 1995–97. Director, Urban Strategy 1993–95. Director of Community Relations, Stanhope 1988–93. Two years at the London Docklands Development Corporation 'learning the regeneration ropes'. Before that – University of Hull (Physics and Philosophy), followed by two years' causing trouble in academe as an elected full-time officer at the National Union of Students.

PART ONE: MISSED PITCHES

UK Regeneration (UKR) was set up in 2010 in response to several challenges, most notably the demise of the British Urban Regeneration Association (BURA). The new coalition government had all but wiped out the then 'regeneration sector'. Snuffing out URCs, UDCs, HMRs, NDCs (don't trouble yourself with what these all stand for, just take my word for it, we'd become pretty sclerotic) and a welter of other triple-letter acronyms to boot. We began UKR mainly as a vehicle to protect the intellectual property of the old BURA (the networks, the archives, the institutional memory) but also in recognition of the fact that BURA had occupied the space between the public and the private sectors. We thought it was worth preserving.

BURA was held in affection and esteem by various leading lights in the property industry; there was a well of goodwill that could be tapped into for UKR. But what to do with this new vehicle? We considered starting another membership organisation but quickly realised that nobody could afford any subscriptions. We then thought about going into consultancy. But I had just been made redundant from my post as Head of Regeneration at CBRE due to lack of business. We toyed with going into publishing and considered buying Lord Heseltine's 'Regeneration & Renewal' from Haymarket, but courage failed.

We started running events, but that was already a very overcrowded market and it didn't take much in the way of observation powers to realise that charging for them was going to cost more than it was worth. It took about six months of this sort of faffing about before the dawning of our real destiny: if we were so smart as to know how sensitive development of mixed-use places in which people can live and work should be done, then why didn't we go out there and prove it? We started to talk to anyone who would listen, mostly senior officers in local authorities, as to whether they had any suitable sites.

We assembled quite a list, mainly of sites that our friends in the public sector would allow us to 'borrow' to talk up our game, whilst we were in start-up mode. If anyone were to call them, they would say they were 'in discussions' with UKR. And that more than sufficed. We continued to respond to all government consultations. We contributed to any relevant think tank discussions. We maintained our own free events programmes, the UKR forums, which allowed us to pick the brains of the brightest and the best. We kept up our editorial submissions for publications such as the *Estates Gazette*. As such, we developed quite a profile. And thus, we came to the attention of Grant Shapps, who was then Housing Minister.

Grant Shapps gave us our first leg-up, giving evidence at the CLG Select Committee in July 2011. He endorsed us by quoting from one of our press releases, which we had issued in hope and hubris: 'UKR aims to provide 20,000 new homes by 2020' after getting provisional backing from Barclays. Once the Housing Minister has endorsed you in public, you begin to give the appearance (at least) of being a real entity. UKR became a living exponent of how you can, indeed, 'fake it, till you make it'.

We had two principals in UKR, me and Paul Evans, as the former chair and vice-chair of BURA respectively. In 2011, we were joined by Jason Blain, a former senior player in the entertainment industry. Jason brought us a wealth of fresh thinking from an industry focused on its public, not itself. Jason was super critical of the dissociative nature of the property industry, as he saw it, particularly the residential sector, who clearly did not give a fig for its consumer.

Housebuilders, he perceived, all but ignored the people who would actually live in their houses. The logic of wishing to do things differently, to have a relationship with our consumers, led us to embrace the nascent PRS market in 2011. We had some reservations, but we could see that the PRS would allow us to develop a brand, some brand values, inculcate brand loyalty and – most of all – put people at the heart of the model. It helped that it chimed with government thinking, then, as now, that institutionally funded PRS could form an important response to the housing crisis. We were beginning to look like a going concern. A PR boost was given by my now co-author, Peter Bill, at that time writing a weekly column for the *Evening Standard*. Peter wrote this short article, published in the London newspaper on 15th July 2011.

Whirlwind, Brains and the Outsider are a winning trio

'An almost audible snort of disdain came from property insiders on July 1 when Housing Minister Grant Shapps endorsed a £3 billion plan drawn up by three outsiders to build 20,000 rented homes. Who are the trio? What kind of thing? Why should they succeed where property companies and pension funds have failed? Why has their company, UK Regeneration, already had offers of eighteen sites from councils that could lead to the building of thousands of homes, 1,500 of them on three large sites in London? Finally, why such disdain? Let's take the questions one at a time.

'The trio: Jackie Sadek? Think Janet Street-Porter, but even wittier. She is a forceful extrovert with twenty years' experience of cajoling abashed men into doing what they are told in order to get highly complex regeneration projects such as Paddington Basin off the ground. Mrs Whirlwind. Paul Evans is the quiet one: a man who escaped from the civil service after twenty-five years to run planning and regeneration departments at Southwark and Tower Hamlet councils. Mr Brains. Mr Outsider is Jason Blain, a forty-one-year-old Scot, who says Sadek is "the talent", perhaps because he comes from the talent management world. The former global head of strategy for Sony Entertainment and BBC Worldwide runs a business investing in music, technology and now, perhaps, property. He arrives with a due sense of wonderment. "The whole process seems to be all about the transaction. There is an almost complete absence as to the value of building a brand."

'*UK Regeneration plans site-by-site joint ventures into which councils donate land in return for a stake. Why? Because a new Shapps law lets them keep the council tax for six years. Barclays has given an open promise to raise at least £150 million. Why? Think of the political pressure it is under to lend. UK Regeneration bothers because Sadek cares and because Blain thinks they can profit from the caution that has kept insiders outside the rented market. That caution surfaced during a meeting of insiders at the British Property Federation last week. Here the consensus was that making the 6% net return from renting the properties is highly unlikely – 'we've all done the numbers, chaps' – even if Barclays does come up with the cash, which the chaps also thought unlikely.*

Blain almost groans, saying the returns have of course been figured out and will be boosted by commercial space on the 500-unit urban sites. He adds: "We are very clear what we want to do, that is to both disrupt the market and in doing so develop solutions that through their disruption act as a catalyst for widespread change. At the moment there is a profound market failure to provide new rented homes. We want to help people to have a better quality of life. It's not all about financial engineering."'

15ᵗʰ July 2011, *Evening Standard*

The power of positive PR! For years after we maintained a link to that article at the bottom of our email correspondence. It gave us a powerful endorsement, but more importantly, it also explained in shorthand that we were outsiders – disruptors. Showing that we thought that things could be done differently – and that we intended to prove it! We loved the fact that it painted us as cartoon characters, like something out of Marvel Comics. By the end of 2011, we were pretty well established. We weren't earning anything, of course, but we were fortunate in that we were all at that time in our lives when we could afford not to, at least for a bit. I had my redundancy pay-out from CBRE, Paul had his civil service pension and Jason was a man of means. However, we were going to have to create a real business.

It is nice to have friends. And we at UKR are very fortunate in ours. Two such are Robin Butler and Nigel Hugill of Urban & Civic – the brothers I'd never had. I had had a long association with the boys in their Chelsfield days, when I'd worked closely with them over two decades on such projects as the White City Shopping Centre (later Westfield London), Stratford (later the Olympics Park), Paddington Basin (later the Paddington Regeneration Partnership) and Merry Hill (later the Brierley Hill Regeneration Partnership). In 2009, they had founded Urban & Civic, an act of great style and chutzpah, with their brilliant purchase of Alconbury.

I'd gone in to see Robin one day soon after the *Standard* piece appeared for a cup of tea. 'Gizza office,' I'd said, only half-jokingly – we may have had a good showing at the select committee and some great PR, but we were now drifting a bit, and we did need a base. It was worth a punt. Bless them, if a couple of days later they didn't then offer to take us in! Robin sent me an email on a Saturday morning saying, 'Nigel and I are agreed that you can squat in one of the offices. But we'll kick you out if any of Hugill's latest musings mysteriously find their way into the EG,' and then Nigel followed up, saying we need a 'promise from JS not to be squawky'. I retorted that I could happily comply with both conditions; well, at least the first one, anyway. And UKR joyfully then moved into the U&C office, where we were kindly provided with a little self-contained suite of offices – two rooms, a tiny kitchenette and a loo – on the ground floor of the building we called 'the Gingerbread House', deep in the heart of the Grosvenor Estate. It was super generous, particularly as they wouldn't take any rent for three whole years. And their team were lovely, particularly their assistant, the super capable and long-suffering Deirdre Taylor.

Never underestimate the power of having such an excellent address! It gave us a great start. Any success that UKR may now have is owed in large part to the generosity of the U&C boys and their team when we were first finding our way. Urban & Civic went on to play a large part in the rest of the UKR story, of course, and are still friends and mentors to this day.

At this point, we were joined by Gill Marshall. I had first met Gill at the London Docklands Development Corporation in 1988 before Canary Wharf was even a hole in the ground. By sheer chance, we met up for a cup of tea and a catch-up halfway through 2011.

Gill had been made redundant from Gateway to London (the inward investment agency for the East side of London) the year before and – like many people at that time, post-financial crisis – was at a loose end. It seemed like a natural move to recruit her to the cause (whatever that was). She originally joined to run the UKR forums – something she still does to this day – but she very quickly became an integral part of the team. Her formal job title was 'Head of Stakeholder Engagement' but we also had some alternative business cards printed up which read 'Gill Marshall, Head of Love and Laughter', which was more than a nod to UKR chairman Jason Blain's belief that the housing industry needed a lot more humanity. It was entertaining to watch Gill at industry events, such as MIPIM, assessing people and deciding which version of the business card to proffer.

Down the wrong road

A long slog down the wrong road began. Years during which UKR worked up ideas on several sites, mainly in local authority ownership. All were in the larger regional cities, such as Nottingham, Derby and Sheffield. London land values really wouldn't sustain the model we were promoting. In every case, the scheme would comprise a mixed-use development, with managed workspaces, community uses, some limited retail under a substantial amount of privately rented homes. All the sites were urban and quirky in some regard. They generally had listed buildings that needed a sensitive response, or a canal frontage, or some such.

The weeks took on a pattern. Every Wednesday and Thursday, Gill and I would be on the East Midlands Line, out of St Pancras to Nottingham, Derby or Sheffield, sometimes with a day full of meetings in the diary, sometimes with not a lot of real purpose other than to establish a physical presence in whatever city we were visiting that day and to keep up forward momentum.

We are urban regeneration practitioners. So, making use of anything a site has to offer is meat and drink to us. We knew about town centre regeneration and how to work in partnership to get government funding for small-scale regeneration projects. We could also draw on a massive amount of goodwill from our suppliers. Many were ex-BURA members, all of whom were seriously decent people who shared our ambition to disrupt the sector. But despite our considerable amount of effort, none of the potential inner-city development schemes came to fruition. It was hugely frustrating.

The main reason was finding funding. But partly that was because there were far too many moving parts. One was the developing nature of the PRS itself. I had been at CBRE during the formative years of PRS when the Urban Land Institute and others had been busy importing the model from the United States. There, PRS is institutionally funded and provides most of the social housing available to less well-off citizens. Successful PRS models depend on developing a brand and having an ongoing relationship with your consumer. People would buy into not just your bricks and mortar, but into your ability to form a community. Since the UKR team understood far better how to create a community than the established property industry, we thought we would be much better placed than anyone else to forge a new paradigm predicated on this model. If only.

Nottingham and Derby

In both Nottingham and Derby, the two most developed UKR projects, we persisted in trying to do too many things. We were trying to put the community first. We were trying to do the right thing by listed buildings. We were trying to do the right thing by all the stakeholders. We were trying to create a mix of uses. We were trying to create an address in its own right. To get any of these things right is hard. To get them all right altogether is almost impossible. Both cities had a well-established 'cottage industry' in the private rental market. But neither of them had anything in the way of an institutional PRS market.

Most of the homes surrounding the Nottingham site were HMOs – Houses in Multiple Occupation. Most were subject of this terrible word 'studentificaton' – they had become student residences. The landlords did very well, as it was lucrative. The students did very well because it was all cheap and cheerful accommodation. But the part of the community it didn't work for was the all-year-round existing residents – the owner-occupiers. People trying to live an ordinary life. For eight or nine months of the year, they would be overrun by the rabble who would leave Kentucky Fried Chicken wrappers in the streets and generally be partying all night. Life was pretty insufferable for them. The council was worried about getting more 'studentification'. When we went in with our PRS model, they slapped us with what is called an Article 4 Direction, which meant we couldn't rent to students.

I kept pointing out that we didn't need Article 4 Direction on what was going to be 320 flats. We could just have it written into a lease that we wouldn't have students. Also, not to put too fine a point on it, we were going to be charging rents that would prohibit anybody other than the richest graduate students. Our planning consultant, Bob Woollard of Planning & Design Group, wrote a long paper for Nottingham City Council explaining how we would prohibit students from living in the units. No good. After we fell out of bed on the deal the (council-owned) site was sold to Persimmon, who would, of course, build houses for sale. There is then no restrictions on owners letting these houses to students.

Sir Adrian Montague

In a timely development, in 2012, Sir Adrian Montague had been asked by the government to form a commission to write a report on the barriers to institutional funding of the PRS. UKR (Paul Evans and me) gave evidence to his commission and, uniquely among those called, said we did not favour government subsidy for PRS, nor a separate Planning Use Class. This rather went against the grain of received wisdom in the market at that time, but it greatly entertained Sir Adrian who – to this day – remains a firm friend and mentor to UKR.

The resulting Montague Commission Report was highly regarded and led to the formation of the PRS Task Force, a group of industry experts who sat within CLG advising on policy. From 2012, UKR continued to struggle with the PRS. The government was showing willing, having set up a task force. We organised for members of the CLG PRS Task Force led by Andrew Stanford, and including Dominic Martin and Tracey Hartley, to visit our Nottingham and Derby sites, together with the leaders of the two local authorities. Funding aid for PRS was made available. UKR dutifully applied to the Homes and Communities Agency.

We went through ten months of due diligence, submitting 150 documents – before being told that we were ineligible due to having no track record as a developer! This goes to the heart of one of the greatest contradictions which lies across many government programmes. The government will say it wants to support disruptors, but nobody is prepared to support someone without the requisite track record. This is public money, of course, so I would hesitate to suggest a glib solution. What I will say is that we were unnecessarily dicked about. In all applications (be they public or private), a quick 'no' never offends.

Hot air

Meanwhile, PRS was spawning more seminars, conferences, think tank reports, policy papers than you could shake a stick at. The authoritative work is still the 2012 Montague Commission Report. The subsequent hot air around the sector and the sheer volume of words, written and spoken, is a wonder to behold. Successes can be pointed to in London and Manchester and one or two other big cities. But PRS had, by 2020, failed to achieve the more widespread traction hoped for. There is a range of reasons for this. Some financial and structural, but some cultural. Let's look at the cultural. There is no doubt that the aspirant British, notably the English, subscribe to a 'property-owning democracy'.

My own family is a textbook case study in this. Both my parents were brought up in inner-city Scotland in rented tenements.

They bought a three-bedroom end-of-terrace house in the London suburbs in the early sixties which, at £3,000, took all that they had. They couldn't afford any furniture, but they took the view, rightly, that furniture would come. They then rode the crest of the property boom, trading up and up throughout the sixties, seventies and eighties. As a result of this, my family are moderately affluent in that we now own and live in properties in suburban London, which we could not afford to purchase today. There is a powerful, almost visceral, wish for UK residents to own their own home. We began to understand that the consumer wants to have their skin in their own game.

Working in government

I started working for Greg Clark in March 2014, when he was based in the Cabinet Office. I'd first met Greg back in my NUS days when he was twenty and a fledgeling student politician at Cambridge University, already a budding 'policy wonk' – super bright and keen to make a difference. I was somewhat older and rougher, having only been at a red brick (and the NUS was more of a bear pit than the Cambridge Union), but he made a big impression on me. From Cambridge, and then the LSE, Greg had developed a career in policy formation, after being stellar at the BBC, before heading up the Policy Department for the Conservative Party at a ridiculously young age. From there he, naturally, became MP for Tunbridge Wells in 2005 and Minister for Planning in the coalition government in 2010.

By 2014, Greg had become Minister for Cities and had created a key team of civil servants who sat between BIS (Dept of Business Innovation and Skills) and CLG (Communities and Local Government) and the Cabinet Office. When he offered me the chance to work with him on his Cities agenda, I jumped at it. I was given the job title 'Policy Advisor, Urban Regeneration'. He had another advisor sitting in his private office – one Lord Michael Heseltine. So, my greatest claim to fame was that I had the same job title as my all-time hero in urban regeneration.

Of course, the big push at that time was the devolution agenda. Greg was determinedly prising the hands of Whitehall off the levers of power – and pushing as much power, responsibility and resources as he could down into cities and towns. And the devolution stuff was meat and drink to me, transferring the approach directly from regeneration, getting people to populate and use the powers they had already. Then, by doing that, earn more power and responsibility. Whether it's Manchester or Birmingham or Cambridge or wherever, it's the civic and business leaders of that place who should be stewarding the growth. And we had a lot of success with Greg's Local Growth Fund.

Housing crisis

But, the whole time, coming up fast as the main agenda was the housing crisis. How to get more homes built. In July 2014, Greg was promoted to Minister of State in BIS, retaining his Cities portfolio, and I followed him into 1 Victoria Street. In May 2015, Greg was again promoted, this time into the Cabinet, as Secretary of State at CLG, and I moved over to his private team at CLG as one of five members of his Extended Ministerial Office. And that was a great experience for me; having been a thorn in the side of CLG all through my working life, I thought I'd be treated with suspicion by CLG civil servants. But, once inside, they realised that I was straight, that I was a resource and that I wasn't a threat, so they welcomed me with open arms.

Officials would give me ammunition to fire questions in meetings. As full time-civil servants, they felt constrained. Two or three hundred civil servants are dealing with new housing in the department, most on the third floor of 2 Marsham Street. Most of the work is to do with housing associations. The National Housing Federation is its biggest stakeholder. They are fairly old-school. There is a sense that 'this is the way we've always done things'. Greg, in his wisdom – and he is the politest man in the world – used to describe them as 'incrementalist'.

That said, during my year at CLG, a wholesale review of the Homes and Communities Agency took place. The senior civil servant who was overseeing the review was a very competent young man, very thorough and intellectually robust. He came to me and said, 'What about the HCA?' I said, 'Just abolish it. It has no plausibility in the market. The brand is toxic. Nobody thinks it is any use.' He said, 'Well... our Housing Minister, Brandon Lewis, has just promised one million new homes by 2020. I don't think we can begin to implement that pledge by abolishing the only housing agency the government has got.' I had to say, 'Well, OK, fair play...'

Homes England

The outcome of his review was a reformatted agency, branded Homes England, which got off to a spectacularly good start – partly because of the appointment of chief executive, Nick Walkley, partly because of the appointment of Sir Edward Lister as founding chairman, who was so good that Boris Johnson hauled him away in the summer of 2019 into No 10 as his chief strategic advisor. Clear blue water was put between the old HCA and the new Homes England. So much so that Theresa May, when Prime Minister, was moved to call it 'the muscular government agency for housing'.

I am in awe of what Homes England has achieved. There has been an enormous change in the culture from the old HCA. Homes England is far more market-facing. Far more 'let's get to solutions' than 'let's find problems'. If you want to make a difference, you have to go and embed yourself in the places that need your support and money. One of the first things Homes England did was make an offer to Deborah Cadman (chief executive of the West Midlands Combined Authority) and Andy Street (West Midlands Mayor) to set up a joint committee on housing supply for their conurbations. Basically, to triage all the sites they had coming through and look at the best way of bringing them forward. Homes England has also done well by inviting suitable private-sector players to enter into agreements that provide tailor-made support – more sensible than simply going out for bids on land, then taking the highest offer. It has also sent a major signal to the industry about MMC, with a splashy announcement in the latter part of 2019 about a strategic partnership with Sekisui House, a large-scale modular housing firm from Japan, and our home-grown housing disruptor, Tom Bloxham of Urban Splash.

In my direct experience, Homes England is innovative and energetic. Although others interviewed for this book have said it can be something of a mixed bag (Chapter Nine), I believe it is – in general – a great force for good. And, at its best, it is quite brilliant.

Biggleswade

By late 2015, I was still working for Greg Clark. I'd always intended to go back to UKR as soon as my sojourn with the government finished. I'd been in Whitehall for more time than I was expecting. Fine, because I hadn't got anything much else to do. But it did seem to me something should come of all that effort put in during five years at UKR. I was beginning to feel that it was wholly untenable to continue to expend my (increasingly in shorter supply) energies on running around the country, telling people what to do from Whitehall. I felt that the only way I could *genuinely* help sort the housing crisis – and, for good measure, whilst we were there, all the other ills of the mainly dismal modern built environment scene – was to get back out there and demonstrate exactly *how* to do it. Show them what good looks like. I wanted to stop talking about it and start doing it.

I gave my thoughts on what might come next to Jason Blain. We had quite a lot of fairly meaningful conversations over the autumn of

2015, one of which was that we had to get back on the horse – and have another go at development. We had learned a lot, put a lot of energy in, and it was unfinished business.

I took a holiday and got home at seven in the morning of November 19th. I had a quick look at my diary and realised that very night I was speaking at an event in Bedfordshire. A former colleague and friend, Ingrid Hooley, had recently moved to Central Bedfordshire Council. Ingrid had asked if I would come and talk about town centre regeneration to the planning authority? I'd said yes, but, blow me down, I'd forgotten all about it. The trains weren't working properly. After a lot of frantic calling around, I got Ingrid to pick me up at Stevenage. She drove me to Central Beds HQ in Chicksands. I was jet-lagged and under-prepared. About seventy folks from eleven town councils would be present. I was looking around as we were driving. It was a dark November evening. But I could see field after field of houses springing up.

Coming up from London

'We have got all these people coming up from London, with small children or starting families, and they're not coming into our town centres. The facilities are just not there. There is no café culture. There is nothing like anything you see in places like Cricklewood or Muswell Hill: from whence the incomers have sold tiny little flats to afford a three- or four-bedroom place in Bedfordshire. They come up here with expectations that we just can't meet,' said Ingrid. 'Our town centres are not good enough for them. We've managed to put together a £4 million fund to help improve our market towns. We are launching it tonight. Can you just give us your thoughts?'

It was a good enough brief for me to build on. I talked about my work with the Grimsey Review into the future of the high street, the need to manage and curate the offer where possible. That we needed to diversify the high street. And that you cannot buy experience online. Standard stuff, really. But new to this audience, and it went down very well. I then got back in the car with Ingrid to be taken back to the station. She mentioned she was renting a house in Biggleswade and said, 'Do you know there is a farm for sale across the road... it's a slam dunk for housing. I was hoping to get it for Central Beds council, but we couldn't get near the asking price.'

Betting on the farms

It took me a little while to digest. But some days later I called Jason Blain and said, 'You know we've been thinking about five-acre urban sites. How about a big urban extension in Bedfordshire?' He said, 'I've been waiting for this call.' We set the wheels in motion. In the event, we ended up buying two adjacent farms, one smaller than the other, giving a total landholding of 960 acres. We didn't have a legal team in place then. But I know Liz Jenkins at Clyde & Co. She fixed up for me to meet the property partner, Robert Pilcher, comfortingly old school, but huge fun. I saw him on 16th December and said, 'Look, I want to buy this farm and I want to exchange by Christmas.' He smiled and said, 'You're a maniac.' We did exchange and complete on the same day, but that day was Friday, February 26th 2016. We paid the full market price for both farms. The first had been on the market for sixteen months. The second farm piggy-backed in on the deal. In stark contrast to our numerous failed attempts to get funding for any of our previous projects, Jason was able to get this one funded in weeks.

Resigning

I knew that I was going to have to resign. On Monday 29th February 2016, I came into the CLG clutching my resignation letter. Greg came in around 10.30 am from Tunbridge Wells, wearing his trademark mac, flapping about, all guns blazing, but clearly in a good mood. I leapt to my feet as soon as I saw him and followed him into his office, saying, 'Secretary of State, can I speak to you about something? It's only going to take thirty seconds.' His private secretary, Alex Williams, sussed that something was up and came bundling in behind me. Greg, wreathed in smiles, said, 'What is it?' I said, 'Do you need to get your coat off – or can you multitask?' I said I'd come to tender to my resignation, that I'd bought a big site and I was going to be conflicted.

By this point, he had sat down at his big long table. He turned to Alex and said, 'This can't happen.' He took my letter and tossed it back to me. 'I don't want this letter. Alex, find the way through. I want Jackie to stay in the department. She can't work in Bedfordshire. Find a workaround.' It was one of the most flattering and complimentary five minutes of my life. We came out and Alex was laughing about it because basically, I'd given them a problem that had to be referred to the Civil Service Commission. It took three months for the issue to go all the way up to Sue Gray, the Head of Ethics and Probity at the Cabinet Office. Sue said, 'Jackie is quite right – she has to come out.' I then worked out my three months' notice and left in July 2016.

PART TWO: HOMES RUN

As we started work on buying the site, we discovered that there was – most fortuitously – an April 2016 deadline for sending in an application to the 'Call for Sites' process, used to help local authorities draw up local plans. I could not be involved in our submission, as I was still working in government. You have to be very careful and divide church from state. But Paul Evans and Ralph Ward, both former civil servants, put together a red-hot submission for the entire 960 acres. That was happily 'deemed to be compliant'. Our submission then started to work its way through the local plan process. At this point in the game, progress seems glacial. It was quite rapid in planning terms, nine months in all. By the time we got around to January 2017, we were in the first draft of the local plan for a portion of the site. This was not a public draft. Six months later, in

June 2017, we were coming up to what's called the Regulation 18 stage – this is when the plan goes public.

By then I'd been working on this full-time for eleven months, since July 2016. But I hadn't been able to talk about it publicly. Central Beds were the planning authority. Their advice was not to put our heads above the parapet. We were beholden to them, dependent upon them. We needed to do it their way and we were not going to fall out with them, no matter what. So, we were good little soldiers.

So, we had quietly got on and did our homework. First, assembling a professional team over the second half of 2016. We'd inherited a lot of goodwill from people who had worked on the Nottingham and Derby schemes. They wanted to work with us again – even though we hadn't been big payers. In fact, in most regards, we hadn't paid anybody very much at all, since we just hadn't got it. In most cases, we'd just about covered people's expenses. But there were more than a few professionals who wanted to remain involved because they believed in what we were trying to do. Thinking we might be proper market disruptors, and that they wanted to be part of the story. They are all thanked in our Acknowledgements at the front of this book.

Master planner

The most important decision we had to make was on the master planner. Stuart Lipton had taught me the importance of a good master planner. Because I've been floating around the industry for so long, an awful lot of people I know might want a crack of the whip. I needed to appoint the master planner in a very transparent, almost public sector way to be above reproach. I asked Paul Finch of the *Architectural Review* to chair a panel that would select the master planner for the whole 960 acres. Paul did a sift of who he thought would be up to the job. We went from his long list to finding eight firms who expressed an interest. Former civil servant Eric Sorensen joined the selection panel. The remuneration for the panel was very modest. We held the meetings in the Soho offices of planners, Quod, under the expert eye of Tom Dobson. We interviewed all eight, then narrowed the list to three by early September: HTA, MaCreanor Lavington and Studio Egret West.

We then told all three they would each be paid £25,000 to produce detailed submissions in two months. I was quite determined to do this in a way that didn't fleece architects. There is this thing that some developers do: getting architects to put a lot of time and energy into things for free. It isn't fair.

In the third week of September 2016, we picked up all the shortlisted team at Biggleswade Station and put them all on a bus and took all them up to the site. It was all very jolly. The sun shone. All seemed to be glad to be in the company of their rivals. As architects do, they took a lot of pictures. We then took them for a pizza. We had given them a well-worked-up brief, which talked about our aspirations, now summed up by the UKR motto, 'everyone deserves better'. Things like introducing more biodiversity than we'd inherited. Disincentivising the use of the private car. A keenness on higher space standards. We were looking for big, spacious homes. We talked about cycleways, walkways, allotments. We talked about decent spaces around the houses. Quite a lot of the site was in the floodplain. We could only develop about 40% of the land. So, we had the potential for a lot of open spaces. We quite quickly got to see that what we were going to develop had to come out of a country park-type setting.

We got three fairly well-worked-up schemes by late October. All three came up with a series of villages across the whole 960 acres. One suggested four villages, another eight villages, the other five. The treatments were remarkably similar. The topography had lent itself to a series of villages. It was at this point we morphed away from what you might call an 'urban extension' into something more like a rural settlement. We held a final set of interviews on 28th October and went with HTA as master planners. One of the things became clear to us during the discussions was that the planting was, if anything, more important than the architecture.

HTA had prevailed – but it was tight, to be honest, we could have gone with any of the three. MaCreanor Lavington and Studio Egret West both produced excellent submissions. But HTA had a very big focus on landscaping. They were hired to work intensively on the plans for the site from November 2016 and we quickly became a coherent team. Needless to say, it did not detract at all, when the principal at HTA and an old friend, Ben Derbyshire, had become President-elect of the RIBA that August. Ben was elected on an agenda of major reform in the architectural profession; just like UKR, he was something of a disruptor. Incidentally, he had been supported in his campaign for election as President by our own Paul Finch. We did begin to feel that we were the Team for Change.

We asked HTA to work within the then-current Central Bedfordshire formula which allows you to roughly calculate the number of homes allowable on the 960 acres. The answer came out as 6,800. We had been thinking 7,000 was about the right number, so, that was fine. But we hadn't started to financially stress test that number. We asked the team to make the houses 25% bigger than current space standards. By Christmas 2016, we had got the whole professional team established. We had appointed PBA (now Stantec) to do the transport and the environmental stuff. We had land-use consultants doing the ecology and biodiversity stuff, and Fairhurst doing the engineering.

Adam Challis of JLL was giving us advice on home typologies. When he sat down to tell me what we should be building, he said to me, 'Now, Jackie, I'm going to say something to you and you mustn't hit me.' He said, 'You are building in what is the middle of the middle of the middle – and there's nothing wrong with that!' I wasn't quite sure how that squared with 'everyone deserves better', but I was glad he was so enthusiastic about the site.

Initial meeting

Our first-ever meeting about this site with anyone not in the professional team or the local planning authority was with Biggleswade Town Council. As soon as we had been allowed to 'go public', we went to them.

We were asked to attend at 7 pm on Monday 3rd July 2017. It was a balmy summer evening. Having thought about it long and hard, we took a team of five. We wanted to show we took it seriously, but we didn't want to pack the room. And we wanted to invoke an informal and accessible tone. Simon Topliss of HTA had produced some excellent boards which laid out the vision in a logical way.

It was quite a tough meeting. We got a fairly cool response at the start. It became clear that the Town Council had not had a great experience with the half-dozen developers who had built up 'Kings Reach' – immediately adjacent to our land – over the past ten or fifteen years. There are over 2,000 homes at Kings Reach. This has helped push up the population of Biggleswade from 15,000 in 2001 to around 20,000 by 2017. And the Kings Reach development is not well integrated into the older, established town. Both sides do, of course, mix. But – we were to learn – generally, 'New Biggleswade' doesn't trouble themselves greatly with 'Old Biggleswade', and vice versa.

It was immediately apparent that the town council felt that they did not have a very good experience at Kings Reach. I guessed that this was, at least partly, because there was no single developer in charge. When these developments were being put into the planning process in the early noughties, the economy was doing well. Then came the financial crisis of 2008. A lot of stuff was then value-engineered to make the sites viable again. That had left some of the development a bit pinched. The road widths weren't good, the tuning circles tight, emergency vehicles found it hard to get through. The verges weren't planted particularly well. It wasn't a layout that you would put forward for an architectural award. A lack of trust in developers, in general, seemed to pervade the town council. And who could blame them? And they were expecting more of the same from us.

Frosty start

The first hour was a bit frosty. But things began to pick up. I made two interjections which I think helped. The first thing I said was that 'anybody who lives in a place is more of an expert in that place than people coming in trying to develop.' I said they were our first choice as to who we were going to meet. So, as far as we can, we are going to be guided by them. There was a bit of a moment when they said, 'Are you agents of Central Bedfordshire?' I had to make it clear also that I was never going to be disparaging about Central Beds. They were the planning authority. We had to work with them. But I wanted to work with the town council; I wanted to be guided by them. I told them they were the experts in the area, and we weren't.

The second thing that helped was when I said, 'I'm not looking for your trust or your support at this stage. Because you can't give it to me. We have not yet earned it. While you are critical of us and holding us to account, that is you doing your job. What you really should be looking for from us is infrastructure first, and second, assurance a place is going to be created that you will like. Because you are custodians of this place.' I do not think it is at all reasonable to ask communities to trust you until you have earned that trust.

We managed to warm the atmosphere in the room a bit, and we certainly had a more positive second hour. It was still one of the toughest evenings of my life. But I came away thinking we'd had a good result but knowing we would have to work quite hard in the future if we were to earn that vital trust. I like to think from what transpired, we did earn the council's trust. But we've never taken it for granted.

I have been asked just *why* we felt we so needed Biggleswade Town Council's trust. They are not the planning authority, after all. But, Central Beds has several market towns to look after, Biggleswade being only one of many and therefore not necessarily a priority. But for all of those town councillors, Biggleswade is *the* priority. They are steeped in Biggleswade. We wanted to be steeped in Biggleswade. We wanted to be in their family.

Community engagement

But, although they are elected, councillors are not the only representatives of the town. So, as of that first night in July 2017, we had gone out on an extensive community engagement strategy under the expert supervision of Gill Marshall, UKR Head of Stakeholder Engagement. We talked to everybody: the Chamber of Commerce, the Rotary Club, Scout groups, local businesses, local agents, everybody. Why is this important, you ask? It's been the guiding force of my career. When I started in property development in the late 1980s, community relations were always seen as a 'nice to have' – the icing on the cake. The analogy of 'cakes' is used a lot: mostly how to 'divide up the cake'. Well, at the risk of stretching the metaphor too far, I believe that if you truly involve the community, you can bake a bigger and better cake. I can still get quite ideological about all this.

I've never really been able to prove that genuine community engagement will create a better product. But I intuitively know it to be the case. At Biggleswade, the council was clear right from the get-go what they wanted. That helped shape the development. By the second or third meeting, we took in quite a lot of their ideas, such as sports facilities and allotments. Our designs had some quite tall buildings; six storeys going into seven storeys in the eaves. We took those buildings out of the scheme.

Traffic jam

But the biggest concern of Biggleswade Town Council, and indeed everyone, was car parking. Cars jammed the narrow roads on Kings Reach in the evenings, when commuters arrived home. When we first started to talk to the planning authority, Central Beds told us to put in three parking spaces per residence. Biggleswade Town Council wanted more. You might think this sounds reasonable. But it isn't just that this is not sustainable; we genuinely believe that all those cars would make for a miserable environment. Without doubt, this is the single biggest challenge that we face in delivering our rural settlement in Biggleswade. And we are not alone: new settlements up and down the country struggle to find sustainable ways of moving people around. We deal with this in more depth in Chapter Four but sadly we do not as yet have the answers. I can't blame both Central Beds or Biggleswade Town Council for pushing for more parking spaces. In places where there are only four buses a day, you can see why people stick with the car. There is no Uber in Biggleswade. There are very few cabs. Everyone is dependent on the private car. We must find a solution.

Build for human needs

Today, the more successful houses, in my view, are not new homes, they are old homes (with some honourable exceptions). Those built to a decent human scale. Volume housebuilders have value-engineered their homes to be smaller and smaller, designing homes that look superficially very attractive. But then you work out that there's nowhere to keep your ironing board. Not enough thought has been given to the way people live. Anyone buying a new build property has to think very carefully about where to keep all their clothes. There won't be enough wardrobe space. There won't be enough space under the stairs. There won't be enough space for toot. Everybody collects toot. There are very few new homes with sheds. The homes at Biggleswade will have 'boot rooms'. The first thing most people do when they come in is take off their shoes and boots. Where do you keep your kids' coats, shoes, bikes, skateboards?

There are, of course, some brilliant examples of well-designed, yet dense, housing developments. People can live in small spaces, particularly in inner-city areas. But we cannot all live in small spaces. A single person can live in a small space. Even a couple without children – or an older person – can. But, once you've got kids, you need somewhere for your children to run. And if you have toddlers you need a house with a garden. All that stuff that we did as kids – go out in the morning with a pack of sandwiches, roam around on your bikes and come back at six o'clock for your tea. None of that happens anymore. Kids are suffering because they're not doing that. There aren't enough places for children to run around and not enough connection with nature. Little children need to commune with plants and soil and little animals. They need to go out and poke at stuff. Little children cannot be cooped up indoors all day; it's not good for them. The coronavirus pandemic has made that clear.

Planning 2018–19

The western quadrant of the site had been allocated for 1,500 units in the Draft Local Plan in the summer of 2017. The late, great, Tony Pidgley of Berkeley kindly came to have a look just to give us some advice and encouragement. I wasn't going to complain about the fact that we had bought at agricultural land value and we now had a quarter of the site allocated for housing. Over the preceding eighteen months our intrepid team of consultants had worked up a planning application. It was to be a hybrid application – outline planning on the 1,500 homes and a detailed component for 240 homes. For the detailed component, we had selected Scottish architects, the Denholm Partnership, led by Jimmy Denholm, as they understood building in a rural context and they were used to building bigger homes than would be usual in middle England. It was about this time that UKR coined our company motto, 'everyone deserves better'.

So, in early June 2018, we duly submitted our application. It had to be loaded onto a planning portal at the local authority and hard copies delivered. With all the supporting documentation, it filled five storage boxes. We were exhausted and we hadn't even started!

We had signed a planning performance agreement with Central Beds at the same time as the submission was lodged. This cost £8,000 a month. After a couple of months, they brought in a truly excellent, highly experienced case officer to work on the application. Biggleswade councillors were still not happy with car parking provision, nor the height of the flats in the detailed application. So, our case officer suggested we withdraw the detailed application and stick with an outline application. We had already done five weeks of community consultations on the hybrid application in the summer.

But another five weeks of consultation was then needed, as the change was considered to be a new application. Thank goodness for Gill Marshall, who patiently sat for endless afternoons in the community centre or the Baptist church. But we were making progress. At the planning committee on 10th October 2018, the development brief for the site, which sets out what sort of place we were trying to create, had been agreed. So, so far, so good.

Statutory bodies

We then get to crunch time with the statutory consultees. Three, in the main, had to be satisfied, the Environment Agency, Network Rail and Highways England. The Environment Agency took a very measured view. Now, this may have been down to our environmental consultants, led by Clare Waller of PBA, who were superb. The Agency wrote a very coherent letter. If we promised to work through a set of detailed steps – such as controlling the flood plain and laying a sustainable drainage system (called SUDS!) – they would be 'minded to support'. An exemplar of how statutory consultees should act.

Network Rail was, I'm afraid to say, not playing a very gentlemanly game. They have a level crossing on the main East Coast Line, over a mile from our site. They would not support any scheme in Biggleswade of more than thirty homes until a £6 million bridge was built over the said line to replace this level crossing. Our lawyers were adamant this was nothing to do with us. But the level crossing is manifestly unsafe and I could see that without coming to an accommodation with Network Rail we were not going to get consent – and we needed consent. Thank God for Homes England – whose remit includes 'enabling sites'. They agreed to include plans for this bridge in their Housing Infrastructure Fund submission. Weeks and weeks of shenanigans, as you may imagine. But at the end of the day, a simple deal was achieved through partnership working on a shared endeavour.

The toughest nut to crack was Highways England. They are almost forced to say no to large scale developments, mostly because all our roads in the South East are already overcapacity. I understand this. But government policy is that we need more homes. The current position is almost always 'the computer says no'. With Highways England, the position was 'if you want to put 1,500 more homes in Biggleswade, the roads won't work'. The first roundabout north out of London on the A1 is just south of Biggleswade. There is a second, north of the town. Highways England said both were at capacity and they could not approve our application. The impasse was eventually broken, again with the help of Homes England, in January 2019.

Planning decision

From then until February 6th 2019, the day of the planning committee meeting, it was pretty well plain sailing. Some of the team, including Simon Bayliss and Andrew Kavanagh of HTA, Ralph Ward, and me from UKR, got the early train. The eastern main line was, of course, not working properly. We were going to be late and I was to be the only UKR speaker at the committee. I took an executive decision and we alighted at Luton and bundled into taxis. It was stressful. Happily, we arrived just on time, at 10.00 am. Chair of the planning committee Councillor Ken Matthews met me at the entrance to tell me that there were to be only two speakers in total – me and the CPRE. I got up and did my three minutes. We got carried, ten in favour, two abstentions. Crucial to this victory was the support of Biggleswade Town Council.

The planning system is what it is: a bunch of technical hurdles that one has to traverse to get consent. At its worst, it's very unimaginative. What you want is a creative planning authority working with the applicant to get a better product. You very rarely get that. What you get is an applicant coming in with their homework. Then the authority marks their homework and gives them, whatever… seven out of ten, 'could do better, please improve'. You end up with a rather anal tick-box exercise. Retail Impact Assessment? Tick (never mind that your scheme doesn't contain any retail, you still need one). Environment Statement? Tick. Statement of Community Interest? Tick. Section 106? Tick. What generally happens is that the application will just be judged simply against its technical merits. Whether it's the right treatment for that piece of land in that location, whether it meets the needs of the local community is secondary to the process. No wonder the planning system ends up with a bad name. Not only is it a bit unimaginative and process-driven, but it can take an awfully long time.

But, I will defend the system and planners to the hilt. We export our planning system all over the world! At the end of the day, they and elected councillors are the only custodians of place we have – the only people looking out for that locality. Planners may have their faults, but they are local and they do at least give a damn! So, I do defend them, even though UKR was a casualty of a system that took nine months longer then it needed to and caused me a lot of undue stress and strain. I will still defend the planning system in the round because they are the people that are protecting us against vagabonds coming in to leg us over and compromise our natural environment.

Got there in the end

And for UKR? Well, we got there in the end. From the purchase of the site in 2016, through getting (part of it) allocated for housing in the emerging local plan, to getting outline planning consent in February 2019 took three years. The industry thought we'd moved remarkably quickly; some of our funders thought the progress was glacial. And, at the time of writing, UKR still hasn't put a spade in the ground. We are working on a reserved matters application but are being blown about by the headwinds of Brexit and COVID-19. But we persevere. I embarked on this journey to prove you could build homes, at scale, at quality, in a place where people wanted to live. And that you could do that without legging over the existing community or compromising the environment. And that you could still make money if you were not too greedy. That is the mission. I would like to create somewhere that endures. That people point to in 200 years. A place that my ghost could come back to and be perfectly comfortable with.

NINE

PUBLIC HOUSES

'There is always an easy solution to every problem – neat, plausible, and wrong.'

H. L. Mencken

In the year to April 2011, just under 40,000 new homes were built for renting to tenants at around half the cost of renting privately. In the year to April 2019, the number of these so-called 'social rent' homes built had fallen to just over 6,000. Over the same period, the number of homes built each year for letting to tenants at 80% of the so-called 'market rents' rose from zero to 30,000. A switch of policy which came about after thirteen years of Labour government was replaced, first by a Conservative-Liberal coalition and then a Conservative majority government from 2015. The net effect of the policy change is a small decrease from 61,000 to 57,000 in the number of what are collectively called 'affordable homes' over the period. Behind these numbers is a more complex story, than just a simple change of policy.

Inside Housing

In May 2010, David Cameron took over as Prime Minister. George Osborne had a mandate to cut public expenditure. One target was housing. What happened was well-described by Pete Apps of *Inside Housing*. 'The fateful decision to move away from social rented housing was taken in the very early months of the coalition government. New chancellor George Osborne was preparing his first major cuts and housing was in the crosshairs. The message to the Department for Communities and Local Government (DCLG) was that the Treasury intended to end state funding for affordable housing.

'Some housing associations might have kept developing, by ramping up their outright sale. But many others would probably have wound down completely. With this threat in mind, it was left to the DCLG to come up with a counter-proposal. What the department suggested was the "affordable rent" regime. This proposal, worked up in a matter of days, was to crank up the rents charged in new rental homes to up to 80% of the market rate. Mr Osborne went for this proposal, cut the housing budget by 60%, and "affordable rent" was born.'

Affordable homes: by tenure, England

Type	2011	2012	2013	2014	2015	2016	2017	2018	2019
Social Rent	39,562	37,677	17,580	10,924	9,331	6,798	5,895	6,679	6,287
Affordable Rent	..	1,146	7,180	19,948	40,860	16,549	24,373	27,084	30,137
Intermediate Rent	4,523	2,055	1,340	1,294	1,105	1,697	941	811	1,401
Shared Ownership					11,128	4,084	9,021	11,084	17,024
Affordable Owner	17,004	17,465	16,975	10,912	3,535	3,486	1,968	1,466	2,636
ALL	61,089	58,343	43,075	43,078	65,959	32,614	42,198	47,124	57,485

Source: ONS

Fall and rise

Halfway through the switch, there was a precipitous fall from 66,000 affordable homes in 2015 to 32,000 in 2016. What happened? Toby Lloyd was head of policy for Shelter for seven years until 2018, when he joined No 10 as a policy advisor on housing. The drop after 2015 was essentially a particularly exaggerated form of the normal effect when one funding programme ends and another begins, plus one key extra detail. In this case, the programme up to 2015 swapped an entirely new tenure – affordable rent – for social rent, which required housing associations to radically change their model.'

Affordable homes built 2015–19

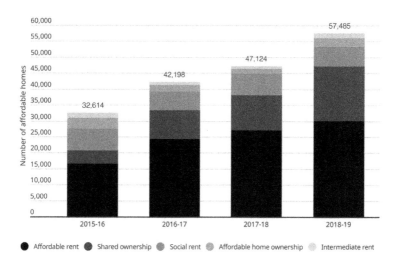

Source: ONS

The raw figures can mislead. In London, for instance, two sub-types of 'affordable rents' were set, below the 80% level, by Mayor Sadiq Khan in 2016. The 'London Affordable Rent,' (LAR) is aimed at those who cannot afford to buy. Pitched just above 50% of local market rents. 'Social rents' in all but name, but still eligible for government grants. Peabody chief executive Brendan Sarsfield has described the scheme as 'social rents, plus a tenner.' L&Q director, Steve Moseley, calculates the average LAR rent in London is 56%, of open market rents. 'Organisations like L&Q peg these rents to local income to ensure they are affordable.'

Next up the ladder comes the 'London Living Rent,' aimed at middle-income folk who want to buy. Rents are set at one-third of gross average earnings on a localised basis and tend to work out at 67%

of market rents. In 2019 the average social rent charged by housing associations in London was £139 per week for a two-bed home. The LAR rent was £158; the 'living' rent £184 a week, against the average market rent of £341.

Making homes affordable again

In early 2020, a 260-page report produced by the self-titled Affordable Housing Commission suggested a major swing back towards building homes that those on low incomes could actually afford. The commission was headed by Lord Richard Best, a distinguished figure in the social housing world with an impeccable liberal record leading the Joseph Rowntree Foundation, before that, as director of the National Federation of Housing Associations. 'Making Housing Affordable Again: Rebalancing the Nation's Housing System' was put together with the help of left-leaning think tank the Smith Institute.

The Best report calls for a reset. Back to 2011 in terms of government grants to allow for new homes to be rented at 'social rents'. Back to the 1970s, with a 90,000-a-year programme to build 'social rent' homes. To help make this happen, government grants to housing associations and councils need to rise from current levels of 15% per unit back to the 50% they were in 2010. Do these things and it will 'rebalance' the housing market by 2045, as 20% of all new homes will be properly affordable. Later in the year the government did promise to spend £11.5 billion building up to 180,000 affordable homes between 2021 and 2026 'should economic conditions allow.' Don't do it, and just 11% of homes will be affordable by then for the poor to rent. A survey by the London Tenants Federation in May 2020 found the stock of social rent homes in London had risen by a net 2,674 since 2004.

The rest of the Best report shows admirable pragmatism. The commissioners are enthusiastic about the growth of the build to rent sector, suggesting tax changes to encourage investors. There is backing for land value capture. 'The commission urges the government to press ahead with the Letwin review recommendations for acquisitions and land value capture through new development corporations established by councils. We recommend the definition of large sites as over 500 homes.' In the summer of 2020 think tank, Localis produced a series of COVID 19-inspired essays (including one from co-author Jackie Sadek) called, 'Building for renewal: kickstarting the COVID-19 housing recovery'. Top of the list were demands to find better ways to capture land value to 'aid and abet' land assembly by local authorities specifically for new towns/villages, using strengthened CPO powers.

Grenfell's shadow falls

The social housing world changed after the Grenfell fire in June 2017. At the Conservative Party Conference in October that year, Mrs May promised an extra £2 billion would be going into the affordable housing pot. But where? A large-scale consultation was launched. Over 8,000 submissions were received and boiled down into a green paper published in August 2018. You can detect the shadow of Grenfell in the Prime Minister's preface: 'Everyone deserves not just a roof over their head but a safe, secure and affordable place to call their own – and social housing has a vital role to play in making sure they do.'

May then signalled council homes may be built. 'Towards the end of the last century council housebuilding virtually came to a halt... but now we need to get back to the scale of new social housing that will deliver a real difference to communities.' Housing Secretary James Brokenshire filled in the details, announcing five principles would now 'underpin a new, fairer deal for social housing residents':

+ A safe and decent home.
+ Improving and speeding up how complaints are resolved.
+ Empowering residents and ensuring their voices are heard.
+ Tackling stigma and celebrating thriving communities.
+ Building the social homes that we need and ensuring that those homes can act as a springboard to home ownership.

Brexit, coronavirus and a 2020 vision for planning

Brexit then engulfed politics. Mrs May's obduracy on the topic saw her eventually resign in July 2019, handing over to Boris Johnson. The Prime Minister's new Housing and Communities Secretary, Robert Jenrick, was supposed to produce a detailed white paper in March 2020. It drew heavily on a January 2020 Policy Exchange report, Rethinking the Planning System for the 21st Century. The author, Jack Airey, became housing policy advisor in Number 10. But the COVID emergency sucked resources away. An eleven-page 'Planning for the Future' was all that could be managed, along with a promise of a 'major white paper' – always a must for any new government.

In June 2020 the Communities Secretary welcomed 'Planning Anew', a selection of essays produced by Policy Exchange, with these words, 'the time has come to speed up and simplify this country's overly bureaucratic planning process", promising the government was "thinking boldly and creatively about the planning system to make it fit for the future. 'I want everyone, no matter where in the country they live, to have access to affordable, safe, and high-quality housing, and to live in communities with a real sense of place. It's time to re-think planning from first principles,' said Jenrick, who, at the time, had been snared into overturning a planning inspector's decision to refuse permission for 1,500 homes proposed by former Daily Express owner, Richard Desmond on the Isle of Dogs. He was forced to rescind, after being caught having dinner with Desmond beforehand.

Boris Johnson had played an earlier part, as Mayor of London, signing off plans for a smaller development of 720 homes at Westferry, once the printworks for the Express and Telegraph newspapers. The Prime Minister promised radical changes in his 'build, build, build' speech on June 30th, as part of a plan to haul Britain out of a post-coronavirus economic downturn. Expectations of radical post-COVID reform were heightened by reports that Chancellor Rishi Sunak, Robert Jenrick and Dominic Cummings, the COVID-shamed chief advisor to Boris Johnson, had formed a troika to think the un-thinkable on planning.

The main changes were set out in Planning for the Future, published in August 2020. (Chapter Three.) Put together during a series of Friday meetings of ministers and civil servants with half a dozen outsiders, including developer, Sir Stuart Lipton, planning QC Chris Katkowski and urbanist, Nicholas Boys Smith. Alongside came a deregulation of use classes, designed to allow high streets and town centres to adapt to changing uses. At the same time a report from retail expert Bill Grimsey, (aided by fellow-author, Jackie Sadek) called for business rates to be replaced by a 2% sales tax. In July 2020 Jenrick introduced new laws intended to 'revitalise town centres.' Full planning consent would no longer be required to demolish or convert unused shops and offices in high streets. In other words, the Permitted Development Rights regime introduced for offices in 2013, would be used, in the Housing Secretary's words 'to re-purpose and help restore our high streets.'

New ministers

Johnson appointed not one, but two, housing ministers. The first, Christopher Pincher, is the well-liked and locally active MP for Tamworth. The second is Stephen Greenhalgh, a former leader of Hammersmith and Fulham council. A jolly character, known for an interest in both housing and cost-cutting. The pair hold joint nineteenth place in the number of ministers since 1997.

Neither should get too relaxed, says Lord Barwell. 'I remember being introduced at the *Property Week* Resi conference in Wales in September 2016 by Lucian Cook of Savills, who I knew from university. Lucian made this gag at my expense. "Let me just run through the timeline of housing ministers for you, Gavin." At the time I had only been in the post for a few weeks. If I had held my Croydon Central in June 2017 – and not ended up as Chief of Staff at No 10 – all I had wanted to do was stay in the job I was in. His message was, don't get too comfortable, mate!'

Homes England

The £70 billion of public money budgeted to cascade into affordable housing between April 2018 and March 2023 pours first from the Treasury fountainhead into a pool marked Homes England. From there it is directed into conduits chosen by the government of the day to water and grow chosen ways of getting more homes built than would otherwise be done so, if the private sector was left to its own devices. In 2018/19, the 870-strong organisation dispersed £857 million in grants to housing associations, used to subsidise the construction of 27,000 homes, about £31,000 per home.

The balance sheet contains a £12.6 billion stake in more than a quarter of a million homes, acquired through Help to Buy. Interest on those loans reaped £56 million in 2018/19. The organisation also owns over £800 million worth of land and property. In 2019, Homes England lent £362 million to finance development and another £284 million in infrastructure loans. The organisation controls a £1 billion 'land assembly fund' and a £5.5 billion 'housing infrastructure fund'.

Bankers, not builders

Mark Prisk is worried. 'My impression is that they've gone from being a developer to becoming a bank,' says the former Conservative Housing Minister. 'They're essentially moving into the provision of finance. People in the financial world say the difficulty is that they've recruited at high-speed, but they haven't recruited well.' Prisk suggests hanging on to public assets and earning income from joint ventures would be better. 'What I want to see is them get a better grip of public sector land. If you and I owned the land, we would go to the private sector and say, "Right, we're going to keep hold of the ownership, but let's agree you develop it and we will draw an income. We may in the future sell it, but we don't want to sell it yet." But the accounting rules and the way the departments operate is that they want to just sell the thing for cash and move away. I think that's not in the public interest.'

Repurposing

The Homes and Communities Agency (HCA) was repurposed in 2018 to become a 'housing accelerator', and renamed Homes England. 'I think the transformation, broadly, has been a good one,' says Lord Barwell. But the former chief of staff at No 10 echoes Prisk's worries. 'People have concerns that Homes England is drifting into doing things the private sector is perfectly capable of doing. The vision we had was to try and use it to unblock sites the private sector found unviable. What I would like to have done, something I was passionate about, was doing deals with councils. To sit down with them and say, "Right, you release the land and, in return, here is money from the Housing Infrastructure Fund."'

Housing associations

Housing associations first appeared in the second half of the nineteenth century, as part of the growth in philanthropic and voluntary organisations brought about by the growth of the middle classes in the wake of the Industrial Revolution. Early examples are the gloriously named Metropolitan Association for Improving the Dwellings of the Industrious Classes, set up in 1841 by George Howard, 7th Earl of Carlisle and a group of aristocratic friends; the Peabody Trust, founded by American financier George Peabody in 1862; and the Guinness Trust, founded in 1890 by the brewing family.

Guinness is still doing good to this day, adding 500 always-well-designed homes to its stock of 65,000 in 2019. Today, Peabody rents out over 56,000 homes, many in those striped-brick walk-up blocks in London. Peabody stands out among housing associations, in the sheer scale of its development ambitions. The association has plans to build 20,000 homes at Thamesmead, to the south-east of London, where it owns pretty much the whole town.

If the public sector had a heart, it would lie in the housing association sector. A big heart, in the sense that consolidation has led to ten giant-sized organisations owning over three-quarters of a million homes. Even the relative minnows swimming along the bottom of *Inside Housing*'s Top 50 own an average 13,000 homes each. What outsiders find puzzling is how few homes they build each year for rent to the poorest quarter of society. Just 12% of the new homes built by the top ten in 2018/19 were leased at a 'Social Rent' – generally half the level of private rents. One third were 'Affordable Rent' tenancies. Well over half the 16,000 homes built by the top ten were sold, either whole or in parts, into the private ownership. Even fewer homes supplied by the bottom ten were leased at 'Social' rents.

Housing association size by completions 2018/19

	Completions	Social	Afford-able	Interme-diate	Low-cost ownership	For sale	Private rent
Top ten							
L&Q	2,862	255	641	29	657	757	523
Places for People	1,876	212	401	34	204	696	329
Notting Hill Genesis	1,856	183	241	0	617	95	720
Home Group	1,660	4	731	0	554	371	0
Platform Housing Group	1,598	458	681	0	459	0	0
Sovereign	1,420	241	639	0	530	70	0
Orbit	1,266	189	544	0	343	190	0
Clarion	1,243	13	641	0	454	135	0
Bromford	1,236	240	501	30	431	34	0
Aster	1,156	156	444	0	453	103	0
	16233	1951	5464	93	4702	2451	1572
% of each tenure		12%	33%	1%	29%	15%	10%
40–50							
One Housing	328	0	93	0	74	155	6
Yorkshire Housing	313	79	102	8	97	27	0
Grand Union	296	9	199	0	87	0	1
Nottingham Community	292	29	168	0	86	9	0
Great Places	281	0	112	0	114	55	0
Green Square	240	43	100	0	93	4	0
Accord	194	0	194	0	0	0	0
Wrekin Housing Group	235	11	163	59	2	0	0
Futures	230	11	73	0	51	7	88
Soha	229	2	169	0	58	0	0
	2638	184	1373	67	662	257	95
% of each tenure		8%	51%	3%	25%	10%	3%

Source: Inside Housing

The sector has been swollen by the acquisition of 1.4 million former council houses over the past thirty years. Associations now own 2.8 million homes across the UK, worth £145 billion. But what might be called 'financialisation' now tends to trump idealism. Associations are now freighted with £77 billion of debt, largely accumulated since 2010, when grants from the government were slashed – a fact that begins to explain why they build so few truly affordable homes.

Network Homes

In 2019, mid-table Network Homes built 480 homes. Just ten were Social Rent. Network came up with an explanation. Building costs have gone up by 42% in ten years and grants have fallen by 66%. Network looked back at seven schemes totalling 404 homes in London and Hertfordshire built between 2008 and 2011. In 2011, it cost £200,000 to build a house – and Network got a grant of £102,000. The association then looked at seven schemes containing 500 homes built between 2015 and 2018 containing 500 homes. In 2018, it cost £285,000 to build a house – and Network got a grant of £34,000.

Places for People

Places for People is more conglomerate than housing association, with a fund management arm and a leisure business. The company owns or manages 198,000 homes. In 2019, they built 212 Social Rent homes. Places for People boasts that it uses 'commercial methods to deliver social outcomes'. The outcome in 2019 was a surplus of £96 million on £4.5 billion of assets – against which lies £3.7 billion of debt.

Notting Hill Genesis

The 2018/19 annual report of Notting Hill Genesis is a model of financial reporting. Nearly 100 pages filled with numbers. Year-end borrowings – £3.4 billion. Reserves– £8.2 billion; 183 homes built for social rent. A total of over 1,400 units for part-sale, private sale and private rent. Notting Hill's highly regarded boss, Kate Davies, has set up a programme to put 'residents at the centre'.

Failing the poor

Former Shadow Housing Secretary John Healey says, 'It's certainly true, particularly in the last five or eight years, some associations have driven much more clearly in the direction of becoming commercial operators. When you make your housing regulator concerned about two things only – one, the health of the financial balance sheet; and two, having professional independent experts on the board and never mind the residents – then nobody should be surprised that this is what happens.'

Former No 10 housing advisor Toby Lloyd defends the sector. 'Housing associations are rule takers, not makers. They respond to government policy, and in every single way their hands are largely tied. They don't have much freedom to manoeuvre. In the last ten years, the government has removed requirements to build social housing – and removed the grants to build it. What do you expect as a result? Today no one builds houses for the poor. In a market system, there's absolutely no incentive for anybody to build an expensive asset for people who can't afford it. Why would you?

'We've seen government mess around with the finances. First, they introduced a ten-year rent settlement, allowing them to raise rents by 1% a year. Vital, because associations then used that long-term security over their income to borrow money. Then in 2016, the government reversed course. Rather than rents increasing 1% per year, they were going to go down by 1% a year. What's the point of having a long-term deal that the government then tears up? The government told them they had to sweat their assets. If anything, the government said they were more often concerned you're not borrowing enough.

'I don't think it's fair to say that that's their fault. They have been actively encouraged. That said, there are still plenty who stay small or local, precisely because it means that they can keep true to their roots. The painstaking, expensive and thankless task of handholding poor and vulnerable people is an expensive business. A lot of associations have been trying to get out of doing that.'

Social value

Hyde Housing Association's Peter Denton is a trained accountant, a former banker and a man who went on to run real estate funds for US private equity fund Starwood Capital. The sort of man that confronted by a tree, you might expect him to wield an axe, rather than hug the trunk. At the Savills event in late 2019, Denton spoke to the uncounted 'social value' provided by housing associations. 'The intangible cost of being in temporary rather than permanent accommodation is high.' Hyde does it's sums. An annual account was put in place under previous chief executive Elaine Bailey. Hyde placed the 'social value' of its services in 2019 at £414 million. Denton said he was lobbying the Treasury to admit social value figures to the government's 'Green Book' valuations of public bodies, the effect of which would be to allow them to borrow more.

How much are social homes worth to society?

The social value of Hyde tenancies	£ million
Economic – more able to work, less absenteeism	186
Health – less likely to have drug and health issues	91
Crime – fewer victims and perpetrators of crime	57
Local authority – temporary accommodation savings	51
Jobs – less likely to be claiming unemployment benefit	15
Education – children more likely to go to school	10
Money – reduction in bank debts	2
Fire – fewer call-outs for domestic fires	2
Total social value	414

Source: Hyde Housing Association

Know your clients

Hyde knows a lot about the 105,000 folks living in the 49,000 homes from regular surveys:

+ 33% are OK financially. Most household incomes are below £30,000; 70% are employed in lower- and middle-income jobs. About two-thirds are tenants, with the remainder being either shared owners or leaseholders.
+ 20% are fifty-five or older but OK financially. While most household incomes are below £30,000, most of this group are rarely in arrears, with around half in employment.
+ 13% are fifty-five or older and struggle financially. Most household incomes are below £20,000 and about half of this group are non-working or retired. Many struggle to keep up with their rent payments.
+ 10% are financially comfortable, with household income more than £30,000. These people tend to be leaseholders or shared owners. Three quarters are employed, with 30% earning more than £50,000.

Lost souls

Nick Raynsford is worried housing associations have lost their souls. 'I have been giving some thought to this recently,' says the former Labour Housing Minister. 'Thoughts prompted by the death of Anthony Fletcher. He was the first director of London and Quadrant Housing Association, at a time when they owned just a handful of homes and operated out of a basement in Deptford.

'Anthony was part of that generation of inspirational people, motivated people, including John Coward and Ken Bartlett, who got the housing association movement back on its feet in the 1960s and seventies. Housing associations disappeared for almost half a century because of the dominance of public sector housing from the 1920s through to the seventies. This inspirational group of people got it back on track and were making real inroads in addressing needs.

'Local authorities had bureaucratic allocation systems and if you didn't fit them, you were left out. Housing associations were able to be more flexible and house people who fell through the local authority net for a variety of reasons. Some had problems which made them unattractive to local authorities, including mental health issues. Some were homeless, at a time when there were no proper obligations on councils to house the homeless. Some black people were excluded by the family and kinship rules that gave priority in some areas to the sons and daughters of existing residents.

'Forty and fifty years on, they have certainly grown. Many have become very large, very bureaucratic, very finance-driven, although some of them are still doing very good things. I still see examples that I'm impressed by. But I think there needs to be a bit of a wake-up call – and getting back to the core mission. If it were me, I would probably insist that they all had local accountabilities – in a way that would ensure that they focused on the needs of certain areas. I think the problems tend to grow when they spread to operating on a national scale, without strong roots in any particular area.'

London and Quadrant director Steve Moseley defends housing associations. 'All the evidence suggests the sector is doing all it can to produce new affordable homes. The homes which are produced still deliver low rents. Supply is just part of the story however and any judgement needs to consider the huge investment needs for the existing 2.4 million homes.

'Everyone agrees that more homes, of all tenures, need to be built and that the current system of development is broken. Government inevitably has a greater part to play here. This needs to involve all players, including local authorities, who now produce a pitifully low output. The crisis in affordable housing is at least in part contributed to by the 2.6 million low rent social homes sold off through the Right to Buy.'

London and Quadrant

The association now tops the tree in terms of new homes built – 2,800 in 2019. L&Q's 95,000 homes are worth £9.5 billion. Since 2015, income has jumped from £518 million to £937 million. Even so, the surplus has fallen slightly from £215 million to £202 million. A big jump in operating costs and higher interest payments on debt that has risen from £2 billion to £5 billion has effectively kept the amount available to spend on development flat.

Grenfell's shadow

Then there is the fallout from Grenfell. At a Savills housing association event in late 2019, the shadow of Grenfell hung like a black flag over proceedings. L&Q's development director Fiona Fletcher Smith said they were spending £30 million a year on recladding, warning 'it is affecting' the new build programme. Her fellow director, Steve Moseley, estimates the final bill for remediation of existing buildings over the next ten years for all housing associations 'could easily top £10 billion, twenty-five times the fire safety funding made available by the government.'

Network Homes boss Helen Evans made it clear at the event where her priorities lay: 'The primary responsibility of the board is NOT to deliver on government housing targets. The safety of our existing customers and dealing with the Grenfell issue comes top. This is bound to have an impact on our capacity of supply. Safety must trump supply issues,' said Evans, who was chair of the G15 group of big London housing associations. The G15 own 1,145 buildings over eighteen metres high, warning that 650 are affected. 'We are talking about years to fix up the existing stock,' said Evans.

In the March 2020 budget, Chancellor Rishi Sunak promised £1 billion of 'Grenfell' recladding grants would be given to both public and private sector owners affected. There was, of course, a catch. 'As a condition of funding, building owners must pursue warranty claims and appropriate action against those responsible for putting unsafe cladding on these buildings, which will be repaid to the government once recouped.' In July 2020 the government made it compulsory for all blocks of flats over eighteen metres high to be inspected for fire safety every five years.

Grenfell fallout

'If we had understood that building regulations were not robust, if we had understood that we can't trust certification, if we had understood that advice was being given from parties who were either specialists or marketing products, was *that* unreliable and misleading… I don't think this tragedy would have happened.' The raw, painful and shameful truth about the UK's weak and compromised building materials certification system finally came to light on March 1st 2020. These words were spoken by a distraught Andrzej Kuszell, founder of Studio E Architects, the practice which had designed the recladding of the Grenfell Tower, which flamed like a roman candle on the night of 14th June 2017, suffocating and burning seventy-two people to death. In May 2020 the practice declared insolvency.

Inquiry

The second phase of the inquiry, chaired by Court of Appeal judge Sir Martin Moore-Bick, had been held up for weeks while the Attorney General, Suella Braverman, ruled on the admissibility of spoken evidence into any possible criminal trials. There were concerns that if witnesses didn't feel they could speak freely, the inquiry would struggle to learn the truth. She permitted the truth to be told.

The first-phase report had already dealt with the fire itself. Now the focus was on who might be to blame for combustible cladding ending up on the twenty-eight-storey block. In the early spring of 2020, almost every day headlines exploded as each of the parties tried to deflect blame, up to the point in March when proceedings were halted due to the coronavirus outbreak.

Meanwhile, housing associations were setting aside hundreds of millions to reclad blocks deemed vulnerable to fire. Private builders who had sold on the freeholds were generally washing their hands. The papers carried stories of owners unable to sell because valuers for the buyer were saying their home was worth literally £0.00 because it did not meet stiffer standards rushed in after Grenfell burned.

The day of the fire, the *Daily Telegraph* asked me for an article. Editing *Building* magazine in the 1990s, I'd observed the close interrelationships between material suppliers and organisations such as the British Board of Agrément, set up in 1966 by the government to provide fitness for purpose certificates. Nothing corrupt. Just the former frequently supplying staff and board members to the latter. An enclosed group, which had no outsiders, no consumer groups to say, 'Hey! Is this safe?' My experiences were reflected in the *Telegraph* article:

'On April 29th 2012, a forty-storey residential tower in Dubai burned like a Roman candle. Four similar fires have lit up the night sky in the Arab emirate in the past five years, the most spectacular being the 2015 New Year's Eve blaze that saw the skin of a sixty-three-storey hotel burn in a way familiar to those who witnessed the way the flames spread up Grenfell Tower. What is similar, in my opinion, between the Dubai fires and the reclad twenty-four-storey council block in West London is this: all were covered in the same type of skin, a yucky sandwich of sheet aluminium containing a flammable filler of rubber or plastic.

'After the first two fires in Dubai, these Aluminium Composite Panels (ACP) were banned in the United Arab Emirates. The London fire makes it almost certain that sandwich panels like these will never again be used to provide a cheap overcoat for old council blocks. Why were they used in the first place? Because they keep the rain out, some heat in – and make the place look a bit more cheerful. They have, of course, been tested for fire safety, so nothing like the fire that has just happened was supposed to happen. As builder Rydon says: "The work met all required building control, fire regulation and health and safety standards."

'I was in the building trade when Ronan Point collapsed in 1971. I was editor of Building magazine in the early eighties when fires in timber-framed homes were highlighted by World in Action. The panel system used to build Ronan Point met the standards of the time. Those early timber-frame homes were also fully tested and approved by the now-privatised Building Research Establishment. Why were these flammable panels approved? Because the fire tests that manufacturers need to pass involve putting up a few panels in a wooden crib and applying a match.

'So why are seventeen people dead [the very early figure]? Get someone drunk and I expect this might be the confession. "Look, Peter, nobody wants to rock the boat. We are all professional people of good intent. We take our job seriously. But, you know, the whole testing *system is controlled by those who pay – the manufacturers. Even back in the day of Ronan Point, they drove through dodgy products that made them money. You can't have some dull guy from the Consumers' Association sitting in on the act and stirring up trouble. We're not bad people, you know. I did say that, didn't I? We have the best of intentions."'*

15th June 2017, *Daily Telegraph*

No justice in New Zealand

Sir Martin Moore-Bick will no doubt cast blame where it should fall. The biggest shake-up of the way building materials are accredited, specified and installed is already underway. But if injured parties think they will gain justice in the form of monetary recompense, they may be disappointed. The lessons from New Zealand's 'Leaky Homes' scandal provides a warning. The regulatory and inspection regime in New Zealand was based on that of the UK. Just like the UK, the New Zealand government thought commercialisation was a good idea. The powerful timber lobby managed to persuade everyone that New Zealand had a Mediterranean climate – and that two-skin cavity walls were a bit of a waste of money. Why not just one skin? And no need to pressure treat the timber with expensive and carcinogen-containing preservatives. When I paid a visit to my sister in Auckland in January 2010, the scandal was gripping the nation. Let me finish with an edited version of what I wrote for *Building* magazine on my return:

Leaky Homes scandal

'Two days before Christmas, the New Zealand government released an explosive report detailing the $11.2 billion (£5 billion) cost of a construction scandal that has left the nation with up to 89,000 leaky and rotting homes, built between 1992 and 2002.

The PriceWaterhouseCoopers document calculates the disastrous financial consequences of the introduction of laissez-

faire building regulations in the early- and mid-nineties. Strict prescriptive codes were replaced with "performance-based" standards after heavy pressure from the construction lobby. The new codes scrapped the need for cavity walls. Timber-framed single-skin external walls, clad with flat cement fibreboard, were allowed because tests showed the method "performed" – by keeping out the rain. Even then, disaster could have been averted – if it were not for the abandonment of timber treatment in 1995 after the powerful timber suppliers lobby persuaded the government it was not necessary. So, the rot set in, literally.

'Who pays? One of the leading cladding suppliers is Australian firm James Hardy. They are defending each case, arguing that if builders had followed the instructions in the product literature, then their cladding would not have failed. Housebuilders? Most have declared themselves bankrupt to avoid claims. Architects and designers? Those affected have gone into liquidation – and set up under other names. The private building inspection service? Their level of insurance was hopelessly inadequate to cope with this disaster. Those affected have gone out of business. But the government is still denying any legal responsibility and is resisting calls to pay 10–15% of the weatherproofing costs to homeowners who drop legal claims. That leaves the local authorities, who have been assailed by claims. They are now being battered into paying 15–25% of repair costs. That leaves homeowners with no builder to sue and to pay the lion's share of the repair costs. That means many owners are currently pretending they don't have a problem. They do; their houses are unsellable.'

February 2010, Building magazine

TEN

EVERYONE DESERVES BETTER

Jackie Sadek

The backhanded compliment 'your heart is in the right place, Jackie' often comes my way. Implying my head is in the wrong place. 'Better to think inside the box, Jackie. Better to be hard-headed, Jackie. Better to be pragmatic than idealistic, Jackie. We're not in the business of building a better society, Jackie, just houses. Don't worry so much about others, Jackie. Stop banging your head against the wall, Jackie. Think of the money, Jackie. Be sensible.'

Sod that. When the co-founder of UK Regeneration, Jason Blain, coined the strapline 'everyone deserves better' for the UKR company motto, it was both a heartfelt plea on behalf of ordinary people and a downright howl of indignation at the dysfunctional and mediocre nature of the housing industry. We have a housing crisis: a crisis of quality and a crisis of quantity. Like the poor, it is always with us. And, seemingly, nobody has the answers.

The better-off can buy better. That is pretty much exactly what anyone with money does when it comes to buying houses. After location, the more money you have the more space you buy. The current non-obligatory space standards are mean, pinched and have barely changed for a century. The grid of standards needs updating, made far more generous and, critically, made mandatory to provide better homes for those who cannot afford to simply buy space. Theresa May put it well in a swansong speech to the Chartered Institute of Housing in 2017.

'I want to see changes to regulations so that developers can only build homes that are big enough for people to actually live in. I cannot defend a system in which some owners and tenants are forced to accept tiny homes with inadequate storage, where developers feel the need to fill show homes with deceptively small furniture, and where the lack of universal standards encourages a race to the bottom.'

Mrs May might have screwed up Brexit. But, my goodness, did she get it right on housing. She finished her speech with this: 'I want to see an end to the era of too-small homes that keep the housing numbers ticking over but are barely fit for modern family life.' Anticipating the moans of those who fear for their residual land values, she ended with this: 'I reject the argument that such a change will make building less likely. It will be up to my successor in Downing Street to deal with this.'

Parker-Boris

Come along Boris. You practically invented the Parker Morris + 10% rules when ruling London by railing against 'homes for Hobbits'. How hard can it be when ruling Britain to impose Parker Morris + 25% on the rest of the country? Just lock the door of No 10 to land speculators and do it. While you are there being Churchillian, impose a grid of maximum densities for new homes. The last twenty years have seen the open-air life squeezed out of housing estates as densities have soared, leaving what's left of the space for cars and vans. I know that parking is a real issue, and we try to deal with that in Chapter Four. Some think we should provide as much 'on-curtilage' parking space as the customer demands (P. Bill). But the majority of right-thinking folk know that we are trying to future-proof development. All expert opinion suggests car use is set to decline. You can argue that once you have sold out the development, the future is for someone else to worry about. But that's not really why I went into this business.

Who builds

In certain parts of the UK (although by no means all) we are simply not building enough homes. And we haven't been for decades. The two main 'providers' – speculative housebuilders on the one hand, and housing associations on the other – are not providing enough homes at affordable prices in the right places. Housebuilders dance to the tune of the economy – and have pushed numbers up hard since 2012. Come any recession that will change. It is a myth that private sector housebuilders are in the business of housing the nation (or at least those that can afford it). They are not: they are in the business of realising a return to their investors.

Similarly, it is a myth that housing associations are in the business of building new homes for the (less affluent) of the nation. They are not: in reality, they build very little themselves and are mainly in the business of managing their existing stock, picking up new housing stock mainly from Section 106 social housing obligations (which is, by its nature, limited). In 2019, the top ten housing associations acquired or built just over 16,000 new homes. Not bad, I suppose. But under 2,000 of those were let at 'social rents' – generally 50% of the market rent, outside London at least. Proof enough they are not the answer to the crisis.

Together – without bringing new players onto this field – they constitute a broken housing market. It is important to recognise that both these models do work on their terms, for their universes. The private model works very well indeed. But they give us only part of the solution. They cannot – and will not – ramp up delivery of homes just because a housing minister gets on their hind legs at party conference and waves their arms, glibly promising 'building more homes'.

Currently, housebuilders are the pantomime villains. You only had to open a national newspaper to read of scandals like Jeff Fairburn of Persimmon trousering a whopping £75 million bonus on the back of 'Help to Buy' (that's OUR money, screamed the British taxpayer, justifiably) or Taylor Wimpey wriggling around, trying to minimise the damage they had done to buyers by selling off freeholds with escalating ground rent clauses. Did they and the other housebuilders who joined this game think beyond the up-front money to the down-the-line damage to their reputation? An Englishman's home is supposed to be his castle, for crying out loud (forgive the sexism). You don't sell customers a castle, then someone else the land.

And in the saloon bars of middle England, the folklore proliferates; tales of shoddy new homes, leaking roofs, poorly tiled bathrooms, guttering coming away, are legion. Photographs are circulated on social media of banners hanging out of windows saying 'Don't Buy Here' or of sides of houses painted with long lists of snagging problems. Architects and the rest of the 'bien pensant' go on record in symposiums vehemently criticising poorly laid out estates.

Sanctimonious associations

The housing associations are rather open to criticism too, despite – or perhaps because of – their somewhat sanctimonious stance. It is rather difficult to maintain your self-righteous position as being on the side of the angels when you have merged and merged into giant behemoths, and you pay your management vast salaries. It's rather unedifying to see the senior teams and boards of these organisations (a metropolitan elite, if ever there was) pontificating about the lives of the poor. And it was a wasted opportunity that the housing associations, with their deep reserves and preferential borrowing ability, did not become a more potent part of the solution over the last twenty years.

Worse still was to witness the flurry, most prevalent earlier in the last decade, for housing associations to ostentatiously enter the private rented sector and for-sale market (perhaps that was them trying to become part of the solution?) only to then behave as rapaciously, if not more so, than their counterparts in the private sector. Thankfully most have subsequently retreated to the core business of minding tenants.

They are all beholden only to a subset of their universe (their boards, the 'Nat Fed', the Ministry and so on) and not even to their residents, really, and it is high time that we gave up the lazy supposition that they will solve the problem of affordable housing.

That said, some are doing some truly excellent work. Some of the smaller regional players in particular still hold to their social conscience. Some are being innovative and smart. I am particularly taken with the approach of Hyde Housing. Not that they are building that many more new homes than their peer group. Rather because they are attempting to introduce the concept of 'social value', putting a price on the benefits of decent housing in terms of the costs to society of folk living in temporary accommodation.

There is a parallel to be drawn here with the private sector, in the sense that you can cost the 'social value' of building decent-sized homes at twenty to the hectare as opposed to housebuilder-sized homes at thirty to the hectare, as demonstrated in Chapters One and Two. Go back to the residual land value numbers for the 1,500 mythical homes in Chapter One (£16 million) and the 2,000 in Chapter Two (£43 million) on the same 100-hectare site. The 'social value' cost of building bigger, more widely spaced homes is, therefore, £27 million. But that's perhaps an argument for geeks (P. Bill). Sod it, I say. People just deserve better.

Housebuilders differ

Not all speculative housebuilders are the same. Some are good, some are not so good and some are diabolical. But all have strengths that can be played to if encouraged. A director in one of the more decent strategic-land players described one of the big four housebuilders as, 'a first-class operator with a very good customer service history and reputation. We may not like what they look like, but they don't tend to get much else wrong.' There are worse criticisms.

Many housebuilders are acutely conscious of their image and are making remarkable efforts to clean up their act. But they are all beholden only to their shareholders, and they should be far more upfront about that. It is high time they stopped allowing people to think – whether it's Her Majesty's Government or the public at large – that they are in the business of housing the nation. That is a convenient untruth perpetrated by housebuilders running in and out of No 10 and No 11 lobbying to protect Help to Buy.

Answer to housing crisis

If the answer to the housing crisis is not the private sector housebuilders, nor the housing associations, nor yet a combination of the two, then what is it? Council housing? Who is going to do the work? A retired chief architect at a council in the north told me: 'There are two events that should never have happened: the abandoning Parker Morris space standards and the handing over social housing to housing associations. We are the poorer for these perceived economies. I have worked on both sides of the line over the years and still feel angry. It is the poor sods at the bottom of the heap who suffer most, and all unnecessarily. At the time I retired, the government was not appointing building professionals any more. And it was left to pea-brained politicians to destroy an amazingly well-integrated range of operations.' Well said, Mr X.

The last time the UK housing market was – more or less – functional was in the 1970s, after councils all over the country had, post-war, embarked on massive housebuilding projects and before Mrs Thatcher implemented Right to Buy, one of the two most popular housing policies ever adopted by the Conservative Party (the other being Help to Buy). Right to Buy was – and continues to be – a success among those fortunate enough to benefit.

But a big mistake was made by not hypothecating the receipts back into funding more housing supply. Lord Heseltine is most eloquent on this, pointing to it being the single biggest failure of housing policy in his political lifetime. And it was very short-sighted of the Conservative Party: by all means, give people capital and they might well become capitalists. But for goodness' sake, build more homes; repeat the process and give more people capital. Or else don't be surprised if you don't have as many capitalists in the future!

One rather noble proponent of council housebuilding is George Clarke, in his 2019 eloquent Channel 4 series *Council House Scandal*, which has done an excellent job in raising awareness. In recent years it has become fashionable to call for the return of wholesale council housing. This is Labour's answer, of course – now. In the interests of balance, it must be pointed out that there was no effort made to resurrect widespread council housing by the Blair/Brown administration of 1997 to 2010. If and when they return to power, it will, of course, provide a partial answer. But I'm forced to conclude that, whilst we believe there is a role for local authorities in facilitating new housebuilding, we cannot see a time when councils will ever again directly deliver homes. The likes of the borough engineer, the borough architect and the borough surveyor will never be seen again.

Old new model

Instead, we should be focused on creating the conditions whereby public and private sector organisations could steward the delivery of good-quality housing stock. What did we have before we had council housing? Going back further in history, to seek for good models of high-quality, popular and locally affordable homes, we naturally come across the private sector 'model villages' built to house workers in places like Port Sunlight, Bourneville, New Lanark and Saltaire.

We look at the old estates build by the likes of Guinness and Peabody, all philanthropic models. So, it can be done; it was done. But who is going to do it now? At this point, we unabashedly put forward the model (eventually) pursued by UK Regeneration. And we are not alone. UKR has joined a band of newish 'stewardship' operators in the housing market, the best being the likes of Urban & Civic and Grosvenor. There are signs that this market is expanding: a potential new entrant to the market is Greycoat, who are renowned for being long-term and gentlemanly operators ('my word is my bond' types) in the London office market. These are all firms that want to buy land outright, keep it for the long term, then put out serviced plots to the market. It is what might be termed a 'stewarded housebuilding model', tended either by the public or private sector.

But this way of working will have to find a new narrative for itself, as we need to make a stark contrast here to the old 'strat-land' operator (author's note: always be chary of any term coined by the property industry, particularly if it is two words conflated; it generally means they're up to no good), guys who have been working up their model for the last twenty years. These people don't even buy land. They tend to have thin balance sheets and they badger planning authorities, trying to winkle out which land might be included for housing in future local plans. Then they take options.

Flip merchants

Housebuilders have been doing this forever, of course, but at least with a view to building houses. These 'strat-land' operators have only short-term intentions. The deal is: you take an option on the land, you get consent, then you flip the land. These people call themselves 'land promoters'. But it's not really about being a promoter, is it? It's not about building homes, is it? There is a big job needed, perhaps by the local government association, to build capacity in the local authority sector to distinguish the difference between those trying to make a turn on the land and those who genuinely want to build homes. Urban & Civic or Grosvenor or UKR are in good faith. But many land promoters coming through the door of planning departments are not. They do not have the interests of the local authority at heart.

Stewardship model

Happily, Knight Frank was already working hard on defining how a new 'stewardship' model would work at the same time as *Broken Homes* was being written. Charlie Dugdale of that parish produced a couple of deep-dive reports into the practicalities in two studies commissioned by government to underpin the rather light findings of the 'Living with Beauty' report. Let Charlie tell it, as he does at the end of Chapter Two. 'We need to help public bodies pool their land with private landowners for long-term schemes and we need to encourage competent long-term stewardship, or trusteeship, of the land. The public sector needs to 'lead the way on this.'

Now, you could argue this 'stewardship' thing is old hat. Sometimes the old ways are the best. But some things need fixing to make them work more effectively in a current context. Charlie again: 'The main issue for private landowners is tax. If they sell to a housebuilder, proceeds are treated as Capital Gains Tax and tithed at a maximum of 20%. If they put the land into a "stewardship" model, the eventual proceeds are taxed as income – which can mean at 40% – double the amount of simply selling. Treasury help is also needed to allow the public sector to put land into the wrapper. Public bodies are obliged to sell land for what's called "best consideration". In short, for the highest price. This guidance needs to be changed to allow public landowners to "invest" their land in "stewardship" partnerships. This would change the landscape.'

Dysfunctional government

Beware. A recurring theme throughout *Broken Homes* is the dysfunctional nature of government when it comes to developing policy, the latest being the Planning for the Future white paper, published in August 2020. I am not going to argue against the idea of Whitehall imposing housing targets, though the almighty rows that will bring are predictable. Nor am I against the rather good idea to base the new Infrastructure Tax based upon the transaction prices. Anything to get rid of CIL and Section 106. But, please do not attempt planning reform unless you are going to do it properly (which these proposals certainly are NOT). And in any case, rodding the planning drains will only ever improve the flow, not the quantity of new homes, a figure determined by the laws of supply and demand, not political wishful thinking.

There are very intelligent people in government to this day deluded enough to think that 'changing the planning system' will magic more homes.

Don't take my word for it; I was only on the inside for a couple of years. Three former housing ministers, one who went on to become Chief of Staff at No 10 agreed in interviews for this book. Just to ram home this scary thought, let's repeat what Mrs May's top man, Gavin Barwell, had to say to us: 'The way in which the government seeks to reach a collective agreement on these things can be completely dysfunctional.'

There is only one thing for it...

Magic wand time

If the coronavirus pandemic has taught us anything, it's taught us the full meaning of the words spoken by Judy Garland in *The Wizard of Oz*. A tearful Dorothy stood in the balloon and clicked the heels of her magic red shoes together three times, as instructed by the Good Witch, and wished herself back in Kansas with the magic words, 'There is no place like home.' On that note, just time to change into my pink Good Witch gown and grab my wand. Now, over what shall I wave it? The first thing would be to find a way around the 1961 Land Compensation Act to allow the purchase of land for housing at existing use value, rather than some laboriously worked up hope value. That is the key. Nobody we talked to disagreed. But, the power in my wand over this topic is limited. You can read the inglorious 100-year history of land value capture in Chapter Five. The laws of unseen complications and unintended consequences wreaked havoc with all attempts. My wand would only be waved over the forty-nine garden communities in which the government hopes 400,000 new homes will eventually be built. No power on earth is going to change things radically on smaller schemes.

Actually, a wand is not what's needed. A gigantic boot up the backside needs administering. Read the miserable history of 'garden community' progress in Chapter Six to see if you don't agree.

Former No 10 housing advisor Toby Lloyd suggests a gentler solution. Take a few of these moribund schemes and make them exemplars. Could that include insisting on 25% bigger homes at lower densities? Toby isn't so sure on density. But – hell yes; the government has the power. That is precisely how I would change the world: not by trying to change every single development from the centre, but by leading with some critical exemplar developments that the government has a big hand in. It is absolutely within the government's power to say, this is how we change the world. Where the government is investing huge amounts of public money, especially for infrastructure and the like, we should be building, not just the average, well, but the best.' My hero Toby, also deserves applause for his report 'New Civic Housebuilding', written while at Shelter. So impressed were the Conservatives, it landed him a job in Downing Street. What did Toby propose? Same as Knight Frank – the stewardship model. Right, where did I put that wand? Oh, here it is!

I wish that:

- Those living in the garden communities would have the pleasure of living in homes 25% larger than national space standards and built no more than twenty-five to the hectare, as was the average outside London at the millennium. Not to the densities of thirty to forty being built today. Note to housing associations and PRS providers: that means you as well.
- Those who own the land would be content with the 'Letwin promise' – to be paid no more than ten times the current use value, as proposed in Oliver Letwin's report in October 2018, and discussed in Chapter Five. This can be paid all at once, or in stages over the life of the development. Leave that to the lawyers.
- The state would retain all remaining surplus land value to pay for what now falls under Section 106 agreements. After all, the state has probably spent unaccounted-for millions in upgrading the infrastructure outside the new community. Save a lot of argy-bargy on 106 agreements.

Last wave

Homes England, at its best, could be a serious force for good in all this. But we stress that it will need to be at its best: be thoroughly strategic, and to move decisively away from 'doing the average, well' as one of their senior directors was recently on record as saying. Gavin Barwell says the organisation has to get 'more transactional', and former Housing Minister Mark Prisk thinks it should stop behaving like a bank. Both think they should stop selling public land to the highest bidder and put said land into either public sector- or private sector-led consortia and take long-term income instead of an up-front cash fix. Agreed.

I'd wave my wand and ask local authorities in designated areas to identify where would be best to purchase land in terms of future allocation for housing under the local plan and to make these known to Homes England. I'd lastly wave my wand over a set of carefully selected private sector companies and ask them to sign up to these principles with Homes England. This would qualify them to be entrusted with Homes England money to go out and acquire the identified land. That would save huge amounts in private financing costs. The payback would be a promise to build a pre-agreed mix of homes to an approved masterplan. The private partner would have to adhere to the principles espoused by the Building Better, Building Beautiful Commission. After all, well, you've guessed the ending to *Broken Homes*: everyone deserves better. Everyone.

INDEX

Illustrations are indicated by page numbers in italics.

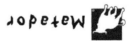

Matador

For exclusive discounts on Matador titles,
sign up to our occasional newsletter at
troubador.co.uk/bookshop